STUFF
STUDENTS
SHOULD KNOW

Learn Essential Life Skills

Dan Marshall

summersdale

STUFF STUDENTS SHOULD KNOW

An Hachette UK Company
www.hachette.co.uk

Summersdale Publishers Ltd
Part of Octopus Publishing Group Limited
Carmelite House
50 Victoria Embankment
LONDON
EC4Y 0DZ
UK

www.summersdale.com

Printed and bound in Malta

ISBN: 978-1-78685-795-8

Substantial discounts on bulk quantities of Summersdale books are available to corporations, professional associations and other organisations. For details contact general enquiries: telephone: +44 (0) 1243 771107 or email: enquiries@summersdale.com.

Disclaimer
Neither the author nor the publisher can be held responsible for any loss or claim arising out of the use, or misuse, of the suggestions made herein.

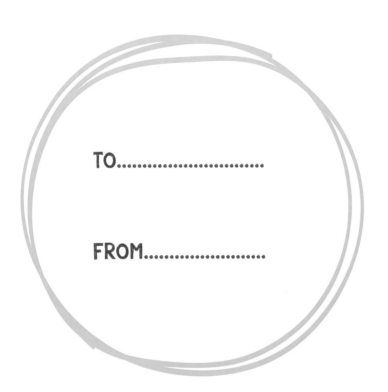

TO...............................

FROM.......................

CONTENTS

6   **INTRODUCTION**

7   **A NEW BEGINNING**

33   **KNUCKLING DOWN**

46   **ACING YOUR EXAMS**

59   **WRITING KNOCKOUT ESSAYS AND DISSERTATIONS**

73   **FOOD FOR THOUGHT**

89   **HEALTHY BODY, HEALTHY MIND**

101 **HOME, SWEET HOME**

128 **MONEY, MONEY, MONEY**

139 **WORK HARD, PLAY HARDER**

167 **GETTING A REAL JOB**

185 **FINAL WORD**

186 **INDEX**

INTRODUCTION

You've worked hard filling out your university application and you've been accepted! So what's next?!

This book is designed to offer the lowdown on university life and the lead-up to it. From finding accommodation to top lecture and exam tips, you'll be the go-to advice giver and number one student know-it-all.

Not only that, this book will also help you transition into a fully functioning adult as you will learn how to cook delicious healthy meals, budget like a pro, and find out what your post-uni options are.

Of course, university isn't all work and no play, so there's a chapter dedicated to fancy-dress ideas, drinking games, and activities to keep you and your friends amused – when you aren't too busy studying and working for some extra cash.

So read on and prepare to become the student who knows all the stuff a student should know.

A NEW BEGINNING

In this chapter you will find out how to:

- Choose the best accommodation for your requirements
- Know what to pack
- Meet new people
- Organise your admin
- Personalise your room

CHOOSE YOUR ACCOMMODATION

Go onto your university website and follow the links to the accommodation information. There will probably be a few first-year halls to choose from and, even though they might look the same on the outside, they will all have different features.

Try to come up with a list of the things you want your new bedroom to have. Although it may only seem like four walls and a roof over your head, there are lots of things to bear in mind. First, work out your spending limit. Second, think about the options that are most important to you. Would you feel more comfortable having an en suite, or are you happy with a shared bathroom? Are you looking to save a little money on accommodation and so would like a roommate, or is it important that you have your own bedroom? Would you prefer the easier life of catered dining, or would you rather cook for yourself?

Once you have made your list, check it against the information in the room advertisements. Obviously you might have to compromise on one or two things as the *perfect* halls sadly don't exist, so working out your priorities will give you a clearer picture when researching your various options.

If possible, attend an open day and take a tour of some of the accommodation on offer. If a room takes your fancy, imagine yourself living there surrounded by your belongings and home comforts. Depending on the university in question, accommodation can be allocated in a variety of different ways: it may be by personal choice, by questionnaire, by a shortlist of your favourite options, or totally randomly. Remember that, wherever you end up, the accommodation team at the university will be on hand to help. If you aren't happy, the staff will offer alternative accommodation. There's often a lot of shuffling around at the beginning of term so never feel like you are inconveniencing anyone. It'll be your home away from home in no time!

Once you've confirmed your accommodation, many universities have an app you can download onto your phone so that you can connect to others who will be in the same accommodation as you. As well as making it easier to break the ice when you first meet them, you can use the app to help you plan who will bring kitchen utensils and equipment to be shared so that you can cut the cost of having to buy everything yourself.

PACK

For anyone who doesn't live a minimalist lifestyle, the main challenge of packing to go to university will be fitting everything into your suitcase or the car boot. Keep in mind that most people overpack when they first move away from home for fear of forgetting something vital. But remember, pretty much all universities are close to shops and city centres so, if you do forget something, it really isn't the end of the world. Try to pack as if you're going on a long holiday and not emigrating permanently!

DOCUMENTS

Let's get the boring things out of the way first. You'll need to bring your important documents with you and keep them safe while at uni. Think about investing in a lockable storage box or a secure filing cabinet. Here's what you'll need to have with you:

- Passport
- Driving licence (if you don't yet drive and need a form of ID for going out, think about getting your provisional licence, as it is far less valuable than your passport if you happen to mislay it)
- University acceptance letter and official correspondence
- Student loan information (so you know what you will be receiving and when)
- Accommodation details and contract
- Bank details and bank card
- National insurance details
- Student discount cards (e.g. 16–25 Railcard, NUS card)

- Insurance documents – if relevant (e.g. health insurance for international students)

- Any important medical information or correspondence, including details of your home GP, to show your new GP at university

SELECT GADGETS

Gadgets are a little more exciting than documents, but these aren't just for fun. Technology is an important part of university teaching and learning, whether you're studying the humanities or the sciences. Don't worry if you don't own a laptop or tablet though, there will always be computers in the library and dotted around campus. There will also usually be university services that can lend you laptops or other necessary technology. Consider bringing:

- Laptop, computer or tablet

- Mobile phone and charger

- Extension cables (don't underestimate how far away the plug might be)

- Memory stick or hard drive

- Desktop printer (not totally necessary but it means you can avoid the queue if you're close to a deadline!)

- Speakers and headphones

- Games console (if that's your thing)

- Adapter plugs (for international students)

NB: Depending on their value, it might be worth taking out some insurance for your various devices. Most rooms provided by the university come with basic contents insurance, but it's important to check beforehand.

STATIONERY

Technology might be important, but the trusty old pen and paper take centre stage during any kind of education. Whatever your subject may be, having some basic stationery in your desk drawer is a must. Pens don't run out of charge and paper can't crash mid-project, so pop into an office supplies store and stock up on colourful bits and pieces to help you organise both your work and your social life. You may need:

- Pens and pencils
- A4 lined notepad (with ring-binder holes)
- A4 ring-binder
- A4 printer paper
- Highlighters
- Post-it® notes
- Calendar/diary (some people find a wall planner showing the whole year to be really useful, that way you can see all of your deadlines and exams at a glance and plan your work around them)
- Paper clips
- Stapler (a must – no essay is just one page long!)
- Sticky tape
- Scissors

FOR THE KITCHEN

Even if you're in catered accommodation, a few mugs, glasses and small plates can be really useful for tea, drinks and snacks. If you'll be cooking for yourself and using a shared kitchen, the most common thing to happen is for *everyone* to turn up with a full set of kitchenware and the cupboards to end up stuffed with redundant pots and pans – since five people simply do not need five colanders! If you're in touch with your flatmates beforehand, try to divide responsibility for bringing the various items between you. If not, bring the bare minimum and work out what you need to buy after the first few days. You may need:

- Cutlery (including sharp knives – you don't want to be chopping with a butter knife!)
- Crockery (mugs, bowls, plates, glasses – enough for one person, and perhaps a few spares)
- Cooking utensils (spatula, chopping board, wooden spoon, cheese grater, bottle opener, tin opener, sieve, etc. – depending on how much cooking you plan to do)
- Saucepan(s)
- Frying pan
- Baking tray
- Oven gloves
- Tupperware containers (for leftovers and packed lunches)
- Washing-up liquid
- Sponge and cloth
- Recipe book (if you fancy being adventurous!)

NB: In university halls, a kettle and toaster are sometimes provided, but if you're concerned about your morning brew, call the accommodation team to put your mind at ease.

FOR THE BEDROOM

Of course you have free rein to personalise your room however you like, accommodation rules allowing, but the important things are:

- Mattress protector
- Duvet and pillows
- Duvet cover, pillow cases and bed sheet (two sets minimum)
- Blankets
- Laundry bag

- Clothes hangers (**Top Tip**: Pack these when you pack your clothes, so you know how many you'll need)
- Alarm clock
- Desk lamp/bedside lamp
- Ear plugs

CLOTHES

This is an obvious one, but there might be a few things you haven't thought of:

- Casual clothes for daily wear
- Smart clothes (even applying for a part-time job requires a job interview)
- Going-out clothes (whether it's clubbing or the end-of-semester ball, you'll want something swanky in the wardrobe)
- Pyjamas, dressing gown, slippers
- Winter coat, jacket, jumpers   ′
- Gloves, hat, scarf
- Shoes (some clubs refuse entry to anyone wearing trainers or flip-flops, so make sure you pack some smart shoes)
- Sports clothes
- Fancy dress (perhaps the most important of all!)

FOR THE BATHROOM

If an en suite awaits, you are one lucky soul! Whatever your bathroom arrangement, you may need:

- Toothbrush and toothpaste
- Shampoo and conditioner

- Shower gel and soap
- Towels (at least two large and two small, so you have a spare dry towel if the one you're using gets too wet or needs washing)
- Wash bag (if your bathroom happens to be down the corridor or you don't want anyone 'borrowing' your shower gel)
- Deodorant
- Flip-flops (communal showers accommodate all kinds of feet)
- Razor
- Wash cloth
- Hairbrush
- Hairdryer
- Toilet paper (just in case your accommodation doesn't provide it)
- Tissues
- Tampons/sanitary towels (even if you don't need them yourself, it's always nice to be able to help a neighbour out in a time of need)

MISCELLANEOUS

- Basic first-aid kit
- Personal medication (together with any necessary prescriptions)
- Basic over-the-counter pain relief
- Glasses or contact lenses (with storage and cleaning kit) and your up-to-date prescription
- Multivitamins (vitamin C is especially helpful for a hangover)
- Contraception
- Backpack (one sturdy enough to hold all those books)

- Small sewing/repair kit
- Matches for candles (if allowed by your accommodation)
- Laundry detergent
- Your favourite books
- Board games
- Bike, helmet and lock (if there will be somewhere safe to store your bike)

TRANSPORT YOUR BELONGINGS

If you or your parent/guardian are unable to drive you to university with the car stuffed to the brim with your belongings, there are plenty of other options available to you.

If you are travelling by train or plane, a large suitcase or hiking rucksack can take the majority of your essentials. If you're really pushed for space, maybe hold off from bringing the bulky things, such as duvet and kitchenware, and buy them when you get there – a sleeping bag will do for the first night or two.

There are plenty of courier services that will collect your luggage from your front door and drop it right at the door of your uni accommodation – just make sure to book well in advance. If you'd rather not send your suitcase ahead of you, it's often simpler and easier to pay by the box load. You can order as many cardboard boxes as necessary really cheaply online (or even ask local shops if you can have the ones that they're going to throw away), and then spread all of your things between them. Remember to tape them up securely and label those that are fragile with a marker pen. Some courier services: Unibaggage www.unibaggage.com, Hermes www.myhermes.co.uk, DPD www.dpdlocal-online.co.uk, Any Van www.anyvan.com.

KNOW WHAT TO EXPECT

Just like school and the wider world in general, people come in all shapes, sizes and personality types. There will be students from every part of the country and many international students from all over the world. It's important to avoid stereotyping people – give them the chance to show you their own individuality.

However, for a bit of fun, you might find people falling into certain 'types' of students:

- **The texter** – Although you're all meant to have your eyes and ears on the lecturer, this student's thumbs seem to be doing overtime, typing away furiously on their phone. It's their own fault if they miss the course material, but let's hope, for your sake, that they have their phone on silent.

- **The walking hangover** – You don't think you've ever seen this student without sunglasses on and without a strong coffee in hand. We might all do it once in a while, but turning up to *every* single lecture in such a sorry state must be bad for their health.

- **The keen bean** – This student's hand is in the air so often during class that you worry for their shoulder joint. We get it, they've done the reading, but do they need to make the rest of us feel so bad about it?

- **The resurrected** – You've honestly never seen them in a single lecture or seminar, but suddenly this student is sitting right next to you in the exam hall. You wonder why some people bother paying the mammoth tuition fees in the first place.

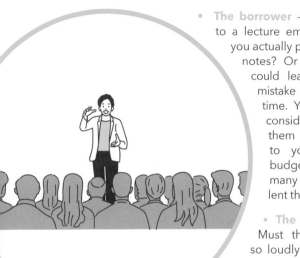

- **The borrower** – Why turn up to a lecture empty-handed if you actually plan on making notes? Or at least they could learn from their mistake after the first time. You're honestly considering asking them to contribute to your stationery budget, given how many pens you've lent this student.

- **The snacker** – Must they really eat so loudly? The lecturer has been drowned out by their noisy chewing.

MAKE SMALL TALK

When meeting new people, the key thing to remember is that everyone is probably as nervous as you are, even if they don't look it. Often, the most confident people are actually the most insecure on the inside. Small talk is the polite, surface-level conversation that we all know and shudder at the thought of, but it really doesn't have to be uncomfortable. Even if you aren't used to it, small talk is easy to pick up and you can soon be chatting away with ease.

The golden rule is: ask people about themselves. Most people love to talk about where they're from and the things they enjoy, and, because it's a topic they know so well, it usually avoids any awkward silences. The three basic questions that you will be sick of saying and hearing by the end of freshers' week are: 'What's your name?', 'Where are you from?', and 'What are you studying?'. Even so, although these questions might get boring eventually, they are an easy way to break the ice and for you both to suss each other out. If you need a new question, consider asking 'What do you enjoy doing?' – it's a great way to get onto more personal topics. You never know, you might have mutual friends in your home towns or a hobby in common. Smile with confidence, be friendly and you can't go wrong. Just try to avoid talking about the weather.

REMEMBER NAMES

It's easy to forget people's names, particularly when you're being introduced to so many new people in such a short period of time. Never be afraid to ask again, as most people will be forgiving. But if you *keep* asking then give these tricks a go to avoid offending someone!

TOP TIPS

Think of an image, rhyme or association connected to that name – maybe a food item that begins with the same letter – and try to imagine it when you see their face. This can help your brain to remember their name when you next clap eyes on them. 'Ah, yes, hello Mr Hamilton', you say, as you see a leg of ham flash before your eyes.

If it's an interesting name, maybe comment on that when you meet them: 'What a cool name! Where does it come from?' The short conversation that ensues could help to fix the name more firmly in your mind.

When you hear a name that's quite common, you're bound to know a friend or celebrity with the same one. So when you meet Dave at football, think of Dave your brother (or whoever) and you'll form a connection in your mind.

An easy one – repeat it back to them. It lets the person know that you're listening and that you care about remembering, as well as giving you another chance to hear the name said aloud. Hopefully this should get those synapses firing!

MAKE FRIENDS

Making friends at university is much easier than you might think. Leaving your school friends behind is tough, but you'll see them again during the holidays. This is an exciting chance to mix with different people from different places and who have had different life experiences. Uni isn't just about academic learning!

Freshers' week is a bit of a blur of hellos, introductions and smiling people, and you might gravitate towards a few different people in those early days, but don't worry if they don't seem like 'your usual people'. Friendship groups shift and change, and you'll find yourself naturally drifting towards the people who really float your boat.

TOP TIPS

Think about bringing a doorstop to uni. By propping your door open in those early days when everyone is anxiously trying to meet new people, you will take away the scary step of having to knock! With an open door, you will seem like an open person and people might drop in for a chat. Plus, once friendships are established, you can *all* prop your doors open and pretend you live in a big studio apartment together.

A cup of tea can go a long way. Even if your neighbours don't have their door open, don't be afraid to knock, introduce yourself and offer to make a hot drink. Maybe you can have a cuppa together and practise your new small-talk skills.

The number one way to meet people that you have something in common with is to join a club or society. Whatever your hobby or passion might be, there is bound to be a group of people that think and feel the same way – you just need to find them! Attend your freshers' fair and sign up to as many things as you think you'd like to try: hockey, baking, dance, drama, chess, rugby, yoga, the list goes on. Just don't do too much otherwise you'll have no time for yourself. Give things a go and pick your favourites based on what you enjoy and the new friends you've made!

GET STARTED

After unpacking and knocking on your neighbours' doors, of course, it's time to get your bearings. Take one of your new flatmates along with you, or simply put on a jacket and head out, whether that's around campus or to your local town or city. This is your new home for the next few years so you'll want to get to know it as soon as possible!

It might sound strange, but going to the tourist information centre isn't a bad place to start if you want to explore your new home. They will have plenty of maps, leaflets and recommendations for things to do in and around your area. Maybe you can put together a list of tourist attractions to see before you graduate?

Next stop is the student union. This is a student-run organisation that represents your views and thoughts in discussions with the university and during the National Conference of Students. It's also responsible for all the clubs and societies at the university – and it can be a nice place to hang out. So take a friend with you and learn about all the things you can get involved with.

ORGANISE YOUR ADMIN

'Adult-y' places, such as the bank and any companies you have direct debits with, need to know you've moved. Important correspondence, documents or deliveries can then be sent to you personally and not build up in a big pile at home. Go online or give the companies a ring to tell them your new address.

Having a local GP is really important, so work out where your nearest surgery or clinic will be and contact them before you start university. They might ask you to come in or send you a medical form in the post. Don't put this off: when you're ill, you really don't want to be stuck waiting in line at a drop-in centre, filling out forms or trying to remember your NHS number. Sort it out as soon as possible so that help will be there when you need it.

STOP FEELING LONELY

Feeling lonely is completely normal. Adjusting to living on your own and being independent is tough – no matter where you are or when you do it. Remember that those around you are probably also experiencing similar feelings; you're all finding your feet in a new town with new people. Give yourself time, and you'll start to feel more comfortable as you relax into your new routine.

If things are still bad after a few weeks, maybe think about joining a new society or club to meet some new people. It's never too late to start something new. Alternatively, speak to a friend at home or a counsellor – and be honest about how you feel. Don't suffer in silence.

REACH OUT.

MAKE YOUR ACCOMMODATION A HOME

When you first move into your university accommodation it may seem a little bare, but once it's filled with your familiar things it will immediately become more homely. Fill your room with anything and everything that makes you *you* – posters, photos, colourful bed sheets, comfy cushions, plants, fairy lights, your favourite books and ornaments. If you want to be reminded of home, think about using familiar colours in your decorations, or familiar smells, such as scented plug-ins.

Having said all this, accommodation contracts can be quite strict when it comes to decorating your room. The near-universal rules are: no Blu-Tack on walls, no candles, and no plug-in fairy lights.

There are plenty of ways to get around these rules without doing any damage or creating any hazards. Always respect the fact that you're only renting the place – your room can still sparkle with personality.

TOP TIPS

Battery-operated fairy lights and imitation flickering candles can help create an ambient glow, without being a fire hazard. But always remember to switch them off when you leave the room!

If you're after sweet smells, try a room spray or a reed diffuser instead of a scented candle.

Washi tape is your new best friend! This coloured paper tape leaves no residue, so you can use it to put up posters guilt-free, or even to decorate boring furniture and bookshelves.

MASTER THE TERMINOLOGY

In any new environment there will be words and phrases that you have to get your head around – it's a little bit like learning a new language. Hopefully this list will get you started!

- **Undergraduate/undergrad:** This is what you are! This is someone who is undertaking their first degree. The 'under' part means that you haven't graduated yet.

- **Bachelor of Arts (BA):** The official title of an arts degree, and what will be on your degree certificate once you have graduated. This includes the humanities, such as History and Philosophy.

- **Bachelor of Science (BSc):** The same as a BA but for sciences. This includes the social sciences. Some departments will have BA and BSc forms of the same subject (e.g. Human Geography is a BA but Physical Geography is a BSc).

- **Postgraduate:** The next step on the academic ladder. This is someone with an undergraduate degree already under their belt. 'Post' means after, so this is the degree you do after you have graduated in the first one. A 'postgrad' will be studying for their master's degree.

- **PhD:** This stands for Doctor of Philosophy, although PhD students can be studying any subject. They will be working on developing their thesis, writing their 100,000-word dissertation, and they may even be teaching some of your classes.

- **Module:** Almost like a class at school, this will be a specific set of lectures and seminars in a particular area of your subject.

- **Course:** Your course is made up of the modules, designed to cover specific aspects of your subject area. The successful completion of your course(s) will lead to being awarded your degree.

- **Credit:** Each module you take will be worth a certain number of credits, and there will be a minimum number of credits that you must obtain in order to pass the academic requirements for each year.

- **Enrol:** At the beginning of the academic year, you will be officially enrolled onto your course and then it will be up to you to enrol yourself onto the modules of your choice. Your uni will tell you how the process works for your particular subject.

- **Contact hours:** The time spent face-to-face with a professor or lecturer (anything outside of this is called independent study). This includes lectures, even though you will be one of many students, and one-on-one meetings with your tutor or supervisor.

- **1st, 2:1, 2:2, 3rd:** This is how university work is marked, just like A, B, C, D. Every assignment you do will fall into one of these categories. Anything below a 3rd is a fail.

- **Faculty:** The teaching staff of a particular department.

- **Single honours vs joint honours:** A single honours degree is a course with just one overall subject, but a joint honours degree is split between two subjects (e.g. French and History), with the student taking modules in both.

- **Plagiarism:** Passing off someone else's work as your own. Even if accidental, universities take this pretty seriously, so don't just copy an article you find online. Research your university's policy on plagiarism and always keep it in mind when writing up your projects.

TACKLE ANXIETY

Anxiety is an emotional reaction; it comes and goes in all aspects of life, just like any other emotion. This is particularly true for students as university can be a stressful time with many different pressures that are new to you. Just remember, if you are feeling anxious about your work, a deadline or a presentation, this is totally normal. The feeling will pass after completing your assignment. But if you're feeling anxious on a regular basis or about things you think *shouldn't* be worrying you, it might be time to ask for some help.

Talk to a student counsellor or your GP and be honest about how you're feeling. They are qualified to help you and can give you some coping strategies to calm you down when you are feeling anxious and worried. Alternatively, go online to www.mind.org. uk and read about anxiety, or contact one of their mental health workers and they will give you some advice on what to do.

REACH OUT IN A CRISIS

If something isn't urgent but is really worrying you, 111 is the helpline for the NHS and 101 is the non-emergency number for the police. In an emergency, call 999 and ask for the appropriate emergency service(s).

If you're having a personal crisis and need to talk, reach out to a friend or your parent/guardian and they will help you as best they can. If you'd rather speak to someone who doesn't know you, call your student helpline and talk to one of their volunteers, who will listen to you in a non-judgemental way. A counsellor or an anonymous listening service, such as the Samaritans, will let you talk as much as you need to without rushing you and without judgement. What is important is to remember: never try to deal with a crisis alone – there will always be someone who can help you.

KNUCKLING DOWN

In this chapter you will find out how to:

- Prepare for lectures and seminars
- Take notes effectively
- Retain information

PREPARE FOR THE START OF TERM

Once you know what your modules will be, your professors might send you a reading list or ask you to buy certain textbooks before you arrive at university. Don't feel as if you have to buy and read every single item on the list immediately. Start by having a look through the compulsory course material, and familiarise yourself with the content that will be covered. If anything sparks your interest over the long summer break, go with it. It will stand you in good stead to have some foundational knowledge before you arrive and having a few useful facts under your belt can't do any harm.

Sometimes course books can come with hefty price tags. Online forums and group chats can be a helpful way of finding second-hand copies of the really expensive books, which older students might be looking to sell on. Look at websites, such as www. AbeBooks.co.uk and www.usedbooksearch.co.uk, to find used copies and avoid paying top dollar. If you're still struggling, email your lecturers and ask them if there is anything the university can do to help. There could be spare copies in the university library that they will reserve for you, or they might be able to help you in other ways.

UNDERSTAND LECTURES

Unlike lessons at school, a lecture can have up to a few hundred people in attendance. Lecture halls are typically full of tiered seating – a bit like going to the cinema – all facing a whiteboard or projector. The lecturer will stand at the front and deliver a presentation on a particular topic, while the students take notes on their laptops, in a notebook, or perhaps by recording the lecture on their phones to return to later. Most lectures last for approximately one hour. Depending on their style, or the topic, the lecturer may pose questions to the room or ask you to interact with the people either side of you. Remember that a lecture won't tell you *everything* there is to know about the subject, since it is only meant as an *introduction* to the topic. Lecturers intend you to go away and research the topic in more depth before starting your projects or attending your workshops, labs and seminars.

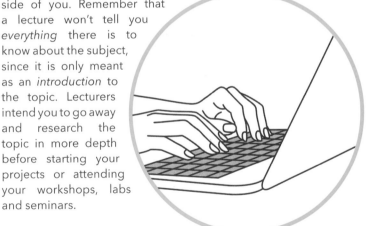

PREPARE FOR LECTURES

Before your lecture you are usually given a brief overview on what it will be about. It's a good idea to research the subject in advance so that you will be able to concentrate on what the lecturer is saying – otherwise you might feel overwhelmed by the amount of information they are relaying to you. Sometimes you will be required to complete tasks or reading before attending the lecture. If you don't complete that task then you're likely to spend a lot of the lecture trying to catch up with or understand what the lecturer is talking about.

Think about and write down the questions you might want to ask in the lecture. If the lecturer covers your query that's great, but if they don't you can always ask them during or after the lecture at an appropriate time.

PACK FOR LECTURES

It's up to you *how* you make your notes – if you make any at all – but whether it's with a laptop or pen and paper, make sure you're prepared. Bring plenty of paper and more than one pen, or a laptop with full charge. You'll be sitting there for a while, so a bottle of water is also a good idea.

TOP TIPS

- When you've got back-to-back lectures, you may be sitting on a wooden bench for most of the day, so don't make yourself suffer any more than you have to. Instead, take a cushion with you to make yourself more comfortable while you learn. If you don't want to lug a cumbersome cushion around with you on campus all day, buy an inflatable one that fits easily into your bag.

- Discreet snacks are OK, but don't become the phantom rustler who is always delving into some snack packaging just as the lecturer is making a fantastic point.

- If you're suffering with freshers' flu, or just an old-fashioned cold, carry a pack of tissues in your bag. The only thing worse than sniffing your way through your lecture is having to leave halfway through to get some tissues.

CONDUCT YOURSELF DURING LECTURES

Be respectful and listen, just as you would when anyone is speaking, but don't be afraid to ask questions. Lecturers welcome interaction and it helps to build a rapport with them if you express an interest in their subject. If you'd rather not disrupt the flow or put up your hand in front of everyone, go up to your lecturer at the end to chat about the things that interested or puzzled you. Most lecturers leave time for this, but, if that's not possible, think about making an appointment to talk to them one-to-one.

Think about the method of learning that best suits you. The most common approach to absorbing information during lectures is to take notes. Some people find that the act of writing down information helps them to remember it. You don't have to take notes, particularly if you find that it distracts you or stresses you out. Sometimes just listening lets you mull things over more clearly – although check that the notes are available on the university's hub so you can revise them later. If you're averse to using notes, but are worried about forgetting some details, perhaps download a recording app onto your phone so that you can make audio notes.

AVOID DISTRACTIONS DURING LECTURES

If you use a laptop in lectures, one of the positives is that you can search for anything related to the topic your lecturer is speaking about. One of the negatives is that the whole world is at your fingertips, including a lot of distracting websites. To make sure you stay focused on the lecture, you can download computer software to temporarily block the websites that send you into the depths of distraction. Most products do cost a small amount, but it'll be well worth it when you pass with flying colours.

TAKE NOTES DURING LECTURES

It is up to you how many, or how few, notes you decide to make, but you will come to realise what's important and what can be left out. Don't try to write every word because it will slow you down – and you'll end up with a set of indecipherable notes as well as having missed parts of the lecture itself.

Jot down the key words and phrases, and any books or sources that you want to investigate further. Use headings, bullet points and abbreviations (see next page) as a good way to condense the most important material. Using a list, rather than a continuous block of words, will make it easier to find information quickly when you return to your notes later.

If your lecturer is waxing lyrical about their time spent researching in the rainforest, for example, you might be able to sit back and listen to the anecdote before noting down a short summary. On the other hand, if they are directly quoting a key thinker, try your best to write it verbatim; but be careful to use quotation marks and add the source so you don't accidentally plagiarise.

TAKE THE BEST NOTES

Take a look around you in a lecture and you will find that a large number of your peers are frantically scribbling every word your lecturer says into their notepads. Use abbreviations instead:

approx.	approximately	sim.	similar
b/c	because	s/t	something
b/4	before	T.	theory, theoretical
c.	approximately, roughly, about (abbreviation for the Latin circa)	w/	with
		w/o	without
		v.	very
		viz.	namely, that is to say
cf.	compared to, in comparison with	vs	against
cp.	compare	≠	does not equal, is not the same as, does not result in
def.	definition		
diff.	different, difference	↑	increase, rise, growth
ea.	each	↓	decrease, fall, shrinkage
fr.	from		
gen.	general	{∴}	therefore, thus
impt.	important	→	leads on to, produces, causes
NB	important, notice this, note well		
nec.	necessary	/	per (e.g. £50/day instead of '50 pounds per day')
pt.	point		
re.	regarding, about		

HANDLE OTHER CLASSES

A seminar is a class with fewer students than a lecture, where the material covered so far can be discussed in a more relaxed environment. These usually take place on more theory-based or thought-led courses, such as English, History and Psychology. A seminar is less about learning the content and more about picking it apart and analysing it. If you are studying a more practical subject, such as Science and Engineering, or Sports, you'll usually attend labs or workshops, where you can begin putting theory into practice. You'll find yourself learning new skills, working with new tools and software, and delving into the practical aspects of your education.

Your session leader will usually send out some work to prepare or a reading to complete beforehand. This is an environment where you can really get into the finer details, discussing your ideas with the professor, the whole group or just a handful of peers. Don't be afraid to ask plenty of questions and to put your own ideas forward. You may get into a few debates, but don't worry – that's all part of academia. Just keep it respectful and listen to the other person. These sessions can be the most useful contact hours because they can help you to really get to grips with your topics before starting your project.

MAKE THE MOST OF SEMINARS, WORKSHOPS AND LABS

Participation is the most important thing: not only does it allow you to make the most of the time itself, but it also shows your academic leader that you really care about your subject. There is nothing worse for a teacher than asking a question to a room full of silent students, so be ready to be the one to answer, even if you haven't fully formed your ideas! You're not being graded, so don't be afraid to make mistakes. That's what this time is for.

If it's relevant, this might be a good time to bring up something from your extra reading. It could add something to the discussion and get the conversation moving if you're stuck in a rut. Try your best to engage and contribute, and you'll find yourself learning from your peers.

If you attend workshops and labs, then get stuck in! You have the amazing opportunity to access equipment and software that costs thousands (sometimes millions!) out there in the 'real' world. Some of the skills you acquire during these sessions will be the bedrock that you build your career on, so make the most of it and say 'Yes!' to every opportunity.

PROCESS INFORMATION

You don't have to remember everything! Reread your notes after your lectures and seminars to make sure that you understand what you've written. You'll surprise yourself by how much you might have written down 'on autopilot', so use this time to trim and edit your notes into a coherent document. If you have the time, making short notes from your notes will help you to pick out the really important stuff. Therefore, when it comes to revising a particular topic, you can consult this short summary and pick out the things you need to brush up on.

Helpfully, a lot of lecturers and professors make their notes and presentations available on the university's portal, which is especially useful if you need some data or a quote that you didn't manage to jot down. You might even have the opportunity to learn it all again, as many institutions upload audio or visual recordings of the lecture, meaning you can watch it as many times as you like. Having access to the portal means it's not the end of the world if you find it difficult to take notes, but don't use it as an excuse to slack off!

ORGANISE YOUR HANDOUTS

Although paper handouts seem to be a dying breed now that most things are uploaded onto university portals, they are great for scribbling extra details in the margins as well as being worth keeping for revision. To keep them in an orderly fashion, so that you can fully benefit from them, try organising them in the following way:

TOP TIPS

- Never stack your handouts in a pile, but buy a concertina (expanding) file to put them in.

- Label each section of the file with the course module name.

- As soon as you get back from a lecture, place the handouts in the correct section of the file, all facing the same way, so they are easy to see.

- Label the handouts clearly and keep them in logical or chronological order within each section.

ACING YOUR EXAMS

In this chapter you will find out how to:

- Revise
- Cope with exam stress
- Eat well during the exam period
- Tackle your exams
- Use your exam time wisely

PLAN YOUR REVISION

Exams are around the corner and you're starting to realise that you should probably stop watching Netflix and start opening those textbooks! When you have a list of subjects, a list of exams, *and* you've just been given your exam dates, it can be hard to know where to begin. A revision timetable is an absolute must. It will help you to get your thoughts in order, use your time efficiently and make everything a little less daunting.

Begin by dividing the number of days you have until your exams by the number of modules or exams you have. This is how many days you have to spend preparing for each one. Now go through each module and make a list of the topics within it that you need to cover. Do this for all your modules and then spread the topics between the days available, giving more time to those that you know are your weak points by taking time away from the topics that you feel most secure on. Write this all into a calendar or a document on your phone so that you can access it wherever you are.

Some people like to split their days into time slots (e.g. revise *Jane Eyre* from 10 a.m. until 12 midday, then revise *Pride and Prejudice* until mid-afternoon). However, you don't need to be too rigid. Writing yourself a to-do list each day, and a separate list to cover the next few days, is an easy way of knowing what you want to achieve and how long you have to achieve it. When planning, it's a good idea to allow some buffers so that if things take a little longer, it's not disastrous. But don't beat yourself up if you don't get absolutely everything done, it's most likely that you've planned too much anyway. Give yourself credit for the work you *do* manage and a pat on the back for being so organised.

REVISE

Create a comfortable but functional environment to revise in. There's no point doing it in a communal area that's noisy, because you'll simply be distracted. Instead, go to the library or sit in your room – (but try not to relax in bed while reading or you might fall asleep!). Know what's right for *you* – if you find it easier to concentrate with some background noise, play some suitable music, whereas if you like silence, it's often beneficial to go to the library.

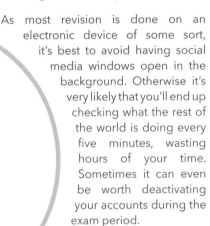

As most revision is done on an electronic device of some sort, it's best to avoid having social media windows open in the background. Otherwise it's very likely that you'll end up checking what the rest of the world is doing every five minutes, wasting hours of your time. Sometimes it can even be worth deactivating your accounts during the exam period.

The examiner won't see your notes so don't bother making them look pretty, although they do need to be neat enough for you to understand what they mean.

- Use highlighters to colour-code different sections of work that link up with other sections.

- Don't try to remember long, overly-complicated sentences, unless you are memorising quotes from sources – but even then it's best to paraphrase.

- Write down keywords and link them to other keywords using arrows, or whatever works best for you.

- Flashcards are great. Alternatively, buy a pack of Post-It® notes. and stick them to your furniture and walls. Make it a ritual that you read them every time you get dressed in the morning, for example, or go to bed at night.

COPE WITH EXAM ANXIETY

First of all, be kind to yourself. Taking days off is very important for your mental and physical health, as studying 24 hours a day will do more harm than good. Try to do activities that get you out of your room and into the fresh air, and involve an element of exercise. Going for a walk in the park (or any nearby countryside) can work wonders for reducing stress. Attend a yoga or art class to keep your mind calm and distracted from worry. Talk to a friend, or go for a coffee, and try to talk about things other than the upcoming exams. Taking a break in this way gives your brain a chance to switch off and you can go back to your desk with a clearer mind.

Most importantly, stay away from people who get you worked up. Whether it's the moaners who tell everyone they're bound to fail, or the cool cucumbers that seem totally on top of their work, you don't want to waste valuable revision energy by getting wound up by your fellow students.

Just do your thing and trust your brain to help you out in the exam room – and in about a month it'll all be over!

COPE WITH EXAM INSOMNIA

Sometimes it seems that your brain is loath to work through the day, then as soon as your head hits the pillow, it activates and you can't switch off.

TOP TIPS

Put away your screens before you go to bed, or at least switch to 'blue light' mode. It has been scientifically proven that exposure to blue light from screens before bedtime disrupts the body's melatonin production, which is essential for restful sleep.

There is usually *some* light pollution when it's time to try to get to sleep. Some of it ycan't be controlled, such as street lights, but make sure that you sleep in darkness, as you're more likely to wake up in the middle of the night if you have left a lamp on. Even TV standby lights can disturb sleep, so always try to turn them off before you get into bed.

The temperature of your room can also affect your sleep. It's always better to be on the colder side than baking hot, so don't leave your radiator on when you go to sleep, as you'll wake up in a dreadful sweat. Ventilate your room by opening your window during the day and, if you can bear the noisy drunks outside, open your window slightly at night.

Rid your mind of your pent-up worries and, if it helps, buy some essential oils for your bedroom to help you to relax. If you find it difficult to stop your thoughts, try visualising a relaxing scene, such as waves lapping or the flow of a waterfall.

STOP FEELING SO SLUGGISH

Remember that a healthy body means a happy, healthy mind. If you're only sat at your desk day after day, then your physical sluggishness is going to be reflected by mental sluggishness. Don't panic if the prospect of the gym sends shivers down your spine! Simply going for a walk in the fresh air, or playing some tennis with a friend, gets you moving and helps to energise your body. The endorphins produced will motivate you to study more productively and will keep your spirits up. If your work is your main priority, then don't view healthy eating and light exercise as a waste of time - you're actually helping improve your productivity and quality of work!

EAT PROPERLY DURING EXAM TIME

Although you might be tempted by treats during those late-night work sessions, avoid relying on sugar and caffeine. Even though they might give you a little boost of energy, it's only short-lived and tough for the body to process. Plus, the comedown can leave you feeling tired and sluggish. Chocolate, crisps and biscuits are out, and vegetables are in. Prepare little 'snack packs' for the day's studying, such as your own mix of Mediterranean vegetables – roasted red peppers, aubergine, olives and tomatoes. Preparing ahead also has the advantage of saving time – your snacks are ready to be munched rather than your having to wander off to prepare another snack (a time killer!).

You need to eat good foods that give you enough energy for the day ahead. Try a bowl of porridge, or toast with peanut butter, to boost you during the morning, and something starchy such as pasta for lunch. Vegetables and grains, such as lentils and chickpeas, will keep your brain at its best for longer. Replace processed snacks with fruit or nuts, which are a natural source of healthy vitamins and minerals that your whole body will need in order to function well.

STAY CALM BEFORE AND DURING AN EXAM

Avoid catastrophising. It's easy to get swept away with worrying thoughts and convince yourself you are about to fail, but you need to stop those fears in their tracks. Try not to talk to your peers about what the exam might entail, as it will probably make your nerves worse – as well as theirs!

Close your eyes and take a deep breath. Remind yourself of all the hard work you've done and let it reassure you that the answer is there in your head. Think of a positive mantra for these moments. For example, 'I know more than I think', or 'I've got this', and repeat it to yourself in your mind. When you feel calmer, open your eyes and smash that exam paper!

I'VE GOT THIS!

START YOUR EXAM

It depends what type of exam you are taking. You'll either be given an 'essay exam', where you'll have to answer one question thoroughly in the allotted time, or there'll be a number of questions you must answer, and they may vary from very short to moderately long.

Where you are only required to answer one question, make sure you read and reread the questions carefully, before you start, so that you understand *exactly* what they are asking. Usually you'll be able to choose from either a broad question on a tricky topic or a specific question, requiring more detail, on an easier topic. Weigh up carefully which questions you think you'll be able to answer and score more marks on. If you're unsure, write a quick plan for both questions, noting what the argument of the essay would be and jotting down an overview of each paragraph. This shouldn't eat into much of the exam time – 5 to 10 minutes maximum. Even if you know straight away which question you want to answer, still write out a plan as it'll keep you on track for the duration of your essay writing. At the end of the exam, draw a diagonal line through the plan so the examiner knows it isn't part of the essay.

If you have to answer multiple questions, don't stop and stress if you don't know the answer to one of them. Instead, look through the paper and answer the questions to topics that you feel confident about. You don't want to get to a question that you could give a brilliant answer to, only to realise you've run out of time. Having a lot of potential points in the bag, so to speak, will make you feel more confident when completing your exam. Once you've answered all your 'easy' questions, go back to the questions you've left blank and split the remaining time between them.

USE YOUR SPARE TIME

Read back through your work. There is bound to be something you could improve or a piece of information you might have missed. If it's an essay subject, rereading your work helps you to gauge whether it's coherent. If you think something could be expressed more clearly, neatly cross it out and use an asterisk to indicate that you will be rewriting that section on another page. Make sure it's clearly marked: you don't want to spoil a good amendment by the examiner being unable to understand where the additional text should go.

If you have answered multiple questions, compare what you've written to the top mark you could receive. If the mark is 5, then usually you'll have to give five valid points to gain them all. If you only have three ideas down on paper see how you can expand on your answers to get the extra marks.

> *you think something could be expressed more clearly, ~~do a good crossing out~~*. Make sure it's clearly marked: you don't want to spoil a good amendment by the examiner being unable to understand where the additional text should go.*
>
> ** neatly cross it out and use an asterisk to indicate that you will be rewriting that section on another page.*

COPE WHEN YOU'RE RUNNING OUT OF TIME

If you're really pushed for time at the end of the exam, try to conclude as best as you can. If you feel like there is more information that you could have included but haven't had the chance to, make a bullet list of the points you would have made. This might sound silly, but it's so much better than leaving something unfinished - and your marker will be reassured that you do actually know your stuff.

TAKE THE NEXT STEPS WHEN YOU THINK YOU'VE FAILED YOUR EXAM

If you think you may have panicked in the exam, or didn't perform to your best for external reasons, speak to the invigilator. They can make a note of illness or stress for the marker to take into consideration.

Wait until you know your actual exam grade, since it could be better than you expected. However, if necessary, you can then contact your department and ask to retake the exam in the summer. The catch is that you will be capped at the pass mark, which is usually 40 per cent, so try to avoid retaking if at all possible.

WRITING KNOCKOUT ESSAYS AND DISSERTATIONS

In this chapter you will find out how to:

- Research an essay subject
- Structure an essay
- Edit and proofread your work
- Plan your dissertation

CHOOSE AN ESSAY TOPIC

What has interested you the most so far? It's always a good idea to write about the things that you're passionate about, since you will be far more motivated to research and read around the topic. That way, it will come across to your examiner that you really have gone the extra mile and engaged with the topic.

Alternatively, choose a topic that you have struggled with. This is particularly good for practice essays that don't contribute to your final grade. You can really grapple with something that you found tricky and get feedback on it in order to improve before it actually counts.

START RESEARCHING SUBJECTS

The reading list is the place to start. Your module reading list will have the core texts on the subject. As you begin to read through the introductory material, you will come across names and thinkers that are relevant to the field. Jot down their names or check the bibliography for texts that take you further into the subject.

The university library will be organised in such a way that when you search for one book, books on similar topics will be stacked near it. So when you go to take the book you want from the shelf, don't leave with it straight away: look along and around the surrounding shelves to find other things that you might not have heard of. You never know, you might find a complete gem.

Of course, the internet is your best friend. There are so many online resources to help with your research. Google Scholar is a good tool, as is your university database, which links you to different academic search engines, articles and journals related to your essay.

PINPOINT THE
RELEVANT SECTIONS

You will never be able to read every piece of information on your subject, unless you devote your life to academia and even then it is likely to be a struggle. After reading the introduction to a topic, work out what is particularly relevant to your essay question. Choose one or two thinkers or books and then read them in detail. Of course you can throw in other titbits of information, but it's usually better to focus on one concept in depth, rather than trying to squeeze in lots of ideas, without developing or expanding upon them.

CARRY OUT
INDEPENDENT RESEARCH

This usually depends on the type of degree you are taking. If you are studying a subject that is built on evidence and data, then it's likely you'll have to carry out practical work. Depending on the information you need to collect, and how you need to collect it, you may have to build projects or carry out experiments, surveys, questionnaires, interviews, case studies, participant and non-participant observation, or observational trials. These practices will help to form the backbone of your essay or dissertation so make sure you give yourself lots of time to plan the data collection – and always remember to explain your methodology.

You'll have lots of guidance in your first year, so don't worry about being thrown in at the deep end for your first couple of projects. A good course leader will make the framework of your individual research clear, including which techniques or methods they want you to use and the results they would need to see in order for your work to be a success.

STRUCTURE AN ESSAY

Every subject and essay is different and each student will have their own methods when essay writing. Most importantly, you need to keep asking yourself whether you are answering the question, or following the title of the essay. If you *do* digress, make sure it's for a reason and that you can link it back to your main argument. But if your writing does go off-piste, it's likely that you won't receive any marks for that section and so it would be worth starting again. Try to think like an examiner as you read through what you've written.

TOP TIPS

- Before you even start to write, ensure you plan your essay properly. Work out what each paragraph will cover and make sure each point in the paragraph can be backed up with evidence or research.

- Don't fall into the trap of making paragraphs unwieldy. Realistically, each paragraph should set out to explore one theme and should be four to five sentences long. This will help to make your essay succinct.

- As well as paragraphs tying together, you want to make sure that the sentences tie in with one another within each paragraph.

- Try to make your work as concise as possible. It's easy to repeat yourself when you want to make sure the reader knows exactly what you are trying to express, but this will only make your work sound clumsy.

- Make sure the conclusion echoes the introduction. Repeat what you set out to do and then discuss what you have established in your essay analysis. If in fact you have not proved or established what you intended, it is equally important to discuss this in the conclusion.

- As long as you don't stray from the essay question and the main aim of your essay, you should be on the right track.

ESSAY PLAN

- *introduction*

- *point one*

- *point two*

- *point three*

- *point four*

- *point five*

- *conclusion*

OVERCOME WRITER'S BLOCK

This is advice for those overachievers who slog away at their tasks even when they aren't getting anywhere. *Walk away from the computer screen.* Honestly, just ignore the project as best you can for as long as you are able. The worst thing for productivity is to stare at a blank screen and hope that inspiration strikes.

Do something totally different. Maybe do something active, meet up with a friend, cook yourself a healthy meal, or listen to a totally unrelated podcast. Engaging with the world around can suddenly spark those ideas and the words will come to you (so be sure to keep a notebook or notes app with you at all times!). When you next sit down at your desk to try again, you'll feel refreshed and energised to give it another go. Next thing you know, you'll be tapping away at the keyboard and your essay will start taking shape.

COMPILE A BIBLIOGRAPHY

Note down every source that you refer to as you go along, even if you don't end up referencing it in the essay itself. This includes websites, articles, journals, books, etc. Once you're done and dusted, check your list against your final essay. You can take out anything that is *totally* unrelated – for instance, an article about a specific idea that you didn't actually use and has no bearing on the argument you made. It might be tempting to keep those titles in to pad out the bibliography, but remember that you want quality, not quantity. A bibliography should demonstrate that you know how to research a topic, which includes knowing when to exclude non-relevant information.

The next step is to put it all into alphabetical order based on the last name of the author, and structure it according to a particular referring style. The most common are Harvard, APA and Chicago, but check with your department which one they prefer.

READ WHAT YOU'VE WRITTEN FROM AN OBJECTIVE VIEWPOINT

Leave yourself enough time to make revisions before you submit your essay. A good way to do this is to put the essay away for a day or two before reading it over. If you try to edit as you go, you will feel so attached to it that you'll find it impossible to cut anything that might not be relevant or useful. Coming back to it after a few days will help you to see it more objectively – as will the person who marks it. Try your best to trick yourself into thinking you didn't write it, and instead imagine you're reading someone else's work. Remember, the marker won't be able to tell that it took you three hours to perfectly craft that paragraph – they'll only be considering whether or not it answers the question satisfactorily.

Failing that, get a friend to read it over and give you their comments. If they understand what you're talking about then you know you've expressed yourself clearly and plainly. Be careful if you're reading over a classmate's essay, as you don't want to accidentally absorb a good point of theirs and put it into your own work. If you do choose to swap essays to check over with someone on your course, make sure the question they're answering is very different from your own.

PROOFREAD YOUR WORK

By writing your essay on a word-processing programme, such as Microsoft Word or Apple's Pages, your work will be automatically spellchecked (as long as you select the correct language of origin in the settings). Alternatively, go online and put your text through a spellchecker. It won't do all the work for you, but it will weed out things that you might not have noticed.

If you are really struggling to get your head around correct grammar usage, think about attending an essay-writing or literacy course at your university. There will be lots of resources to help you get those top marks.

COMPLETE YOUR ESSAY

Read it over from start to finish a couple of times to get a sense of the flow and whether or not you have expressed your argument clearly enough. Give it another check for spelling mistakes and grammatical errors that might have slipped through.

If you have time, ask someone you trust in your department to look it over from the point of view of spelling and grammar. Sometimes this isn't allowed for coursework that counts towards your mark, so be careful not to break the rules. It is always OK to ask a friend or family member to give you their honest opinion. It's still your work so you don't need to take every comment on board, but it's always good to have it checked by someone else.

Once you're happy with it, it's time to submit your work!

START THINKING ABOUT YOUR DISSERTATION

It depends on your subject and when your deadline is, but the summer before your final year is definitely the right time to start thinking about a topic that excites you. Some general research on the subject area itself, which includes finding any key authors or thinkers relating to your dissertation question, will stand you in good stead. It's never too early to give it some thought, as this project will be time-consuming and will require a lot of energy. If you have a burst of inspiration in your first year, write it down! Discuss your thoughts with a course tutor or adviser – they will likely be able to give you some helpful feedback and ask some thought-provoking questions.

Don't leave it to the last minute, as it will undoubtedly stress you out.

FINISH YOUR DISSERTATION ON TIME

Don't leave it too late! You might have heard urban legends about people who wrote their dissertation in a day, but don't even think about trying to be that person. Start early and finish early, with plenty of time to review, edit, and cut or add words where necessary. When you start planning your dissertation, make your own deadlines for the completion of sections and chapters. This way you will know whether or not you are on track for finishing it with time to spare.

Another way to help you stay on track is to book up some one-to-one appointments with your dissertation adviser throughout the third year. In your initial meeting with them, you'll be able to discuss your ideas and receive feedback, and then each time you go back they can offer you further guidance. They should also be able to read a portion of your dissertation and give you some feedback on it before you continue with the rest. This is well worth making time for as it's a good indicator of whether you have the beginnings of a solid argument.

FOOD FOR THOUGHT

In this chapter you will find out how to:

- Store your food
- Prevent waste
- Batch cook
- Avoid empty calories
- Wash up your dishes
- Extinguish a small kitchen fire

STORE YOUR FOOD

Throughout your time at university, you should be prepared for limited living space, including cupboard, fridge and freezer space. University accommodation often means that several people may share one kitchen, but not necessarily share their food or meals (although there's always someone who manages to liberate a few items that aren't theirs!). Everyone needs fair and equal access to the cupboards, fridge and freezer so they can store their food properly. It's best not to go overboard on your food shop, as trying to fit seven ready meals into a freezer compartment may prove difficult!

Every week, look through your quick-to-perish foods: use up anything that is about to expire and chuck away anything that is past its best. At the end of each term (or approximately every three months), have a clear-out of expired store cupboard essentials such as tinned food. If you haven't used something and it's taking up a lot of space, take it to a food bank or swap it with a housemate.

When putting your shopping away, make sure you date-rotate food – just put the item that's going out of date the soonest at the front of your fridge. This will help you to avoid using the food you've bought most recently.

USE LEFTOVERS

Cooking for one is a tricky task, and sometimes almost impossible, but leftovers are great! If they're easily transportable, why not have them for lunch tomorrow and save yourself some money while you're at it? For bulkier meals, your freezer is your friend. A good set of plastic storage containers is a worthy investment. Every time you make a large meal and have eaten your fill, store what's left in individual portions, freeze them, and eat within three months (one month for meat and fish). And *voilà* – you've made your own ready meals!

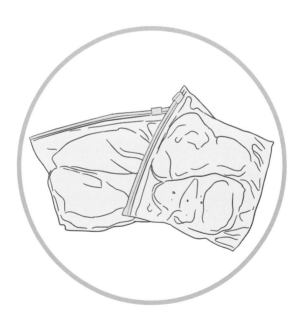

BALANCE YOUR DIET

Of course, it would be easy to eat healthily if each of us had our own nutritional adviser and the money to buy ready-prepared and interesting salads every day. However, being on a tight budget and without having the expert knowledge of someone in the healthy-eating industry, this is a lot harder to accomplish in reality. It's easy for students to get stuck in a noodle-eating monotony, so try your hand at cooking some easy, healthy – and cheap – meals from scratch. Here's a list below to get you started – just search online for them and you'll discover various recipes for you to try.

BREAKFAST

Scrambled eggs on wholemeal toast

Apple and sultana porridge

Baked beans on toast

LUNCH

Lentil and tomato soup

Tuna lettuce wraps

Boiled egg salad

Peanut butter and banana sandwich

DINNER

Lasagne

Spicy three-bean chilli

Tuna pasta bake

Thai green curry

Tofu stir-fry

Shepherd's pie

Cheesy ham and broccoli pasta

AVOID COOKING TOO MUCH

It's hard to judge foods such as pasta or rice by eye as they expand during cooking. This can result in you cooking much more than you expected and some of it inevitably going to waste. Here's a list of the items with the appropriate measurements for one person:

- **Pasta:** Use 70–80 g dried or 100–110 g fresh.

- **Spaghetti:** Measure this with a spaghetti spoon, as the hole in the middle of it is designed to tell you how many dried strands you should be using. If you don't have a spaghetti spoon, 70 g is a good amount for one person.

- **Rice:** If it is the main part of your meal, use 90 g uncooked rice (about half a mug). If it is to be a side dish, e.g. if you are having curry, use 60 g (about one-third of a mug).

- **Couscous:** Again it depends if you are using it as a side or substantial part of your meal, but generally one cup of uncooked couscous is perfect for a main and half a cup is ideal for a side dish.

If you just generally cook too much and it has nothing to do with expanding food, try using a ready-meal container as a template for how much of each food item you should use. Put the uncooked items in the plastic or foil dish, and once filled, you know that you have the correct amount.

BATCH COOK

It's difficult to shop and cook cheaply and efficiently when you're cooking for one. Even the smallest pack of mince feeds two generously so if you're cooking smaller quantities, half the packet can easily end up going to waste in the back of your fridge. Not only that, but sometimes it's worth buying food in bulk as it works out to be significantly cheaper. For example, a 250 g pack of mince may cost £2.25, and a 500 g pack of mince may cost £3.40 – making it cheaper to buy the one 500 g pack at £3.40 rather than two 250 g packs for £4.50. That's a saving of over £1 on this purchase alone – think how much you could be saving overall! The following pages include a number of recipes, all of which can be made in batches and then frozen once they have cooled to room temperature. Then they are ready to be defrosted, heated up and eaten when needed at a later date. Label your stored food with use-by dates, so that you know which food to eat first!

BOLOGNESE SAUCE

Cook up a big pot of this bolognese sauce and divide it into single portions. The next time you're hungry, just cook a portion of pasta for one, add to it a reheated portion of the bolognese sauce, and you've got yourself a bowl of spaghetti bolognese! Sprinkle some parmesan over the top and it'll be as tasty as restaurant food. If you're a vegetarian or fancy a cheaper alternative, replace the beef with veggie or Quorn mince. It tastes very similar and will help both your wallet and the environment.

(Serves four. Prep and cooking time: 1 hour, 10 minutes)

Ingredients

1 tbsp. olive oil

1 large onion, finely chopped

1 garlic clove, finely chopped

1 tsp. dried oregano

1 tsp. dried basil or a handful of fresh basil

2 carrots, peeled, trimmed and finely chopped

2 celery sticks, finely chopped

500 g minced beef or Quorn/veggie mince

400 g tin of chopped tomatoes

1 tbsp. tomato purée

1 beef or vegetable stock cube

Secret ingredient – a splash of red wine!

In a large pan, gently fry the onion, garlic and herbs in the oil until the onion begins to soften.

Add the carrot and celery and keep stirring on a medium heat for another 10 minutes.

Increase the heat and add the mince, stirring for 3-4 minutes until the meat is browned.

Add the chopped tomatoes, tomato purée, stock cube and wine, and stir everything with a wooden spoon. Add a splash of water at this stage if it's looking too dense.

Bring to the boil for a couple of minutes, and then reduce the temperature to allow the sauce to simmer gently. Cover it with a lid and let it cook for 40 minutes, checking and stirring every now and then to make sure nothing is burning.

When you have a thick, rich sauce, season it to taste.

Serve with pasta for one. Cover the rest and set it aside to cool. Once at room temperature, transfer the sauce to freezer-safe containers and freeze in individual portions.

CHILLI CON CARNE

This is a similar process to the bolognese and perfect for spice lovers. This chilli sauce is great on its own or with a bowl of rice and some plain yoghurt. It's perfect for those days when you need some warming comfort food. It can also be made vegetarian with the use of veggie mince rather than beef.

(Serves four. Prep and cooking time: 1 hour)

Ingredients

1 tbsp. olive oil

1 large onion, finely chopped

1 red pepper, diced

2 garlic cloves, finely chopped

1 heaped tsp. hot chilli powder (or 1 tbsp. of mild)

1 tsp. paprika

1 tsp. ground cumin

500 g minced beef or Quorn/veggie mince

1 beef or vegetable stock cube

400 g tin of chopped tomatoes

1 tbsp. tomato purée

400 g tin of red kidney beans

400 g tin of baked beans

Secret ingredient – a few squares of dark chocolate!

In a large pan, gently fry the onion, red pepper and garlic in the oil until the onion starts to soften.

Add the chilli powder, paprika and cumin, and stir, cooking for a few minutes.

Increase the heat and add the mince, stirring for 3–4 minutes until the meat is browned.

Following the instructions on the stock packet, prepare the stock with hot water and add it to the pan, along with the chopped tomatoes, tomato purée, kidney beans, baked beans and cubes of chocolate.

Give it all a good stir and bring it to the boil, before taking it back down to a simmer. Cover with a lid and simmer for 30 minutes, checking and stirring every now and then to make sure nothing is burning.

Season to taste, then turn off the heat and let it stand for 10 minutes. It will continue cooking gently because of the heat – this part of the process is important as it allows the flavours to mingle.

Once the sauce is thick and rich in flavour, it's ready to serve. Cover the rest and set it aside to cool. Once at room temperature, transfer the sauce to freezer-safe containers and freeze in individual portions.

LASAGNE

This is a recipe that involves layering. Use the recipe on page 80 to make the bolognese. Once you have made the béchamel sauce, all that is required are some brick-laying skills.

(Serves four. Prep and cooking time: 1 hour and 15 minutes)

Ingredients for béchamel sauce

300 ml full-fat milk

15 g butter

15 g plain flour

1 nutmeg

Ingredients for lasagne

200 g dry pasta sheets

Béchamel sauce

Bolognese sauce (see page 80 for recipe)

150 g cheddar, grated

To prepare the béchamel sauce:

Bring the milk to the boil and immediately reduce the heat. In another pan, melt the butter until bubbling. Add the flour and quickly stir in, cooking for 1–2 minutes. Remove the pan from the heat and add the milk gradually, stirring until smooth. Return to the hob on a medium heat and bring to the boil, stirring constantly. Reduce to low heat and cook for around 5 minutes, stirring constantly, until the sauce is thick and glossy. Season to taste with grated nutmeg.

To prepare the lasagne:

Line an ovenproof dish with a layer of pasta sheets, then add a layer of béchamel sauce, then a layer of bolognese sauce, then a little of the cheese. Repeat twice. The final layer should be the rest of the pasta sheets, completely covered by the béchamel sauce and the remaining cheese sprinkled on top. Cook for 1 hour at 180°C (350°F).

CHICKPEA CURRY

This is delicious with some rice or naan bread. If you want to save money, buy a packet of rice for boiling as it will go further than the microwaveable kind. But always follow the packet instructions to the letter, as, left to your own devices, the result could be underwhelming to say the least. If you decide to keep any leftover rice, take great care – it can give you food poisoning if not cooled and stored properly.

(Serves four. Prep and cooking time: 1 hour)

Ingredients

2 tbsp. olive oil

2 garlic cloves, crushed

Thumb-sized piece of ginger, grated

1 onion, finely chopped

1 tsp. garam masala

1 tsp. turmeric

1 tsp. ground coriander

1 tsp. cumin

200 g of any combination of these vegetables: tomatoes, spinach, cauliflower (florets), mushrooms (halved), green beans, peppers

400 g tin chickpeas, drained and rinsed

400 g tin chopped tomatoes

400 g tin of coconut milk

In a large pan, heat the oil and soften the onions.

Add the garlic, ginger and spices and cook for 1–2 minutes until aromatic.

Stir in the vegetables and chickpeas until coated and the vegetables have started to soften.

Add the tomatoes and coconut milk and simmer for 30–45 minutes.

Serve on cooked rice, sprinkled with chopped coriander.

DRINK (RELATIVELY) HEALTHILY

We all know that alcoholic drinks have lots of sneaky 'empty' calories in them, but are you aware of how many calories there actually are in different types of alcohol and what they are equivalent to in terms of food? Let's find out…

A large glass of wine (because what student ever goes for a small?!): 228 calories – equivalent to a bagel or a chocolate bar.

A pint of cider: 210 calories – equivalent to a sugar-coated ring doughnut.

A pint of beer: 200 calories – equivalent to a large slice of pizza.

A small 275 ml alcopop: 171 calories – equivalent to a hot chocolate with whipped cream.

A double gin and tonic (two 25 ml shots of gin): 150 calories – equivalent to a pancake or a cup of chocolate-dipped strawberries.

Although wine has more calories in it, it also has a higher alcoholic percentage, which means you probably wouldn't drink as much of it, in terms of quantity, as you would beer, cider or alcopops.

Additionally, non-alcoholic drinks can add many empty calories to your daily intake, with fizzy drinks and milky, syrupy coffees being the worst culprits. Not to mention anything you order with whipped cream on top! If you want to start cutting out high-calorie drinks, try to drink only tea (without sugar) or water (with a splash of cordial if you want to make it more interesting) for five days of the week, and have two days where you can treat yourself to any drink you like.

WASH UP BY HAND

The main things that you need in order to wash up by hand are a sponge, cloth or washing-up brush, and some washing-up liquid.

If you're only cleaning one or two pieces then you can use a small amount of washing-up liquid and get each item done quickly under a running tap with warm water.

If you have a huge pile of dishes to do then fill up the sink with warm water and a larger dash of washing-up liquid to get it full of bubbles. Purchase some washing-up gloves if you don't want your hands to dry out from the washing-up liquid. Rub or scrub things all over with the sponge, cloth or brush, then rinse under running cold water to get rid of the soap suds.

If you have something tougher to wash up, e.g. burnt food on a baking tray, then leave it to soak in some warm soapy water and come back to it in a little while. If it still won't budge, baking soda and white vinegar will dissolve any excess grease or burnt-on food and leave the tray sparkling clean.

PUT OUT KITCHEN FIRES

If the fire is in the oven or the microwave, keep the door closed and turn off the power. If you open the door, the oxygen in the air will make the fire bigger and alarmingly more dangerous. Keeping the door closed will eventually suffocate the flames, but don't just leave it. Keep your eye on it until the flames are out, and if they won't go out, call the fire brigade.

The best tool to combat a fire on a cooking stove is a fire blanket. Rented accommodation and university halls should have a fire blanket on the wall. Read the instructions and throw it on the flames to extinguish them. If it's a really small fire, put a lid on the hob to suffocate the flames and turn off the gas.

Never throw water on an oven top or onto burning oil, fat or grease, as it will only oxygenate the oil and create a large flame. Don't fan the flames either since this will cause them to spread. You want to aim to use a heavy fabric, a wet towel or a fire extinguisher.

If you can't control the flames, **call 999**. If you're in accommodation provided by the university, break the glass on the fire alarm and leave the building. If you are in private accommodation, tell everyone to leave the house.

HEALTHY BODY, HEALTHY MIND

In this chapter you will find out how to:

- Exercise without the gym fees
- Perform basic first-aid
- Assemble a first-aid kit
- Seek advice if you're worried about your health

EXERCISE ON A BUDGET

A gym membership can be a costly investment, and, unless you go on a regular basis, it's a waste of money. But fear not, you don't have to break the bank to get your sweat on! Here are a few cheap or free ways to exercise.

TOP TIPS

- **Go for a run.** This is an obvious one, but you can literally step out of your front door and start getting fit. Remember you need some good trainers and a motivational playlist to keep you going. If your motivation is waning, you could always download a couch to 5K app.

- **Play tennis with a friend.** If you have a couple of rackets and a tennis ball between you, lots of courts will let you play for free if they've not been previously booked – or you could even play in a field. Lay your jumpers and jackets in a long line and you've created a net – just prepare for the imminent arguments about a ball being out.

- **Go to an exercise class.** Although they might be expensive in the real world, exercise classes like Zumba and yoga can be really cheap. Check out the students' union (SU) or some aerobics societies and they'll hook you up with an inexpensive and fun way to work out.

EXERCISE AT HOME

Don't spend crazy amounts of money going to a gym when you can recreate your own gym experience at home with the following exercises:

FOR YOUR ARMS:

- **Towel warm-up:** Warm up your upper body by rotating your arms in circle-like movements while holding the towel. Then warm up your arms by holding the towel with both hands behind your back and slowly moving it up and down.

- **Dumb-bells:** Use unopened food tins or bottled water instead of dumb-bells. Holding one tin/bottle in each hand, lift both arms so they are parallel with your shoulders. Hold for 10 seconds, then lower your arms slowly. Do three sets of ten, with 2 minutes' rest between each set.

- **Strengthening exercises using a sofa (1):** Stretch out your body lengthways, facing away from the sofa, and hold yourself up by placing your hands facing forwards on the sofa. Lower your bum so it's almost touching the floor and lift up until you reach your stretched-out position. Do three sets of ten, with 2 minutes' rest between each set.

- **Pillow power exercise (1):** Use both hands to hold the edges of a pillow and swing it back and forth as if swinging a tennis racket – use a wall to stop the swing, making sure you don't accidently punch the wall with your hand. Do five sets of twenty, with 2 minutes' rest between each set.

FOR YOUR LEGS:

- **Stepper:** Use stairs for cardio workouts or jump squats. Run down them and jump up them, for instance, or see how many times you can go up and down them within a certain time frame.

- **Strengthening exercises using a sofa (2):** Sit on the sofa without supporting your back, then lift your legs off the floor so that they are straight out in front of you. Rotate them slowly in a clockwise movement. Do three sets of ten, with 2 minutes' rest between each set.

- **Sofa or wall lunges:** You can use the sofa to perform half squats by standing on the floor with your back towards the sofa. Lower yourself as if you were about to sit and hover in that position, making sure your back is vertical. Hold this position for 10 seconds. Then gradually straighten yourself back up to a standing position. If you don't have a sofa, support your back against a wall and lower yourself until in a sitting position. Do three sets of twenty, with 2 minutes' rest between each set.

- **Pillow power exercise (2):** Hold a pillow just below shoulder height with your arms stretched out and jump from one foot to the other, lifting your knees high enough so they hit the pillow. Do five sets of ten, with 2 minutes' rest between each set.

PERFORM BASIC FIRST-AID

Now that you share your life with your housemates, you may feel a sense of responsibility for one another. The following techniques are the most commonly used in the event of an emergency. To find out more, visit the NHS web page, which has lots of advice.

WHAT TO DO IF SOMEONE IS UNRESPONSIVE BUT BREATHING

If a person is unconscious but still breathing, perform the following steps:

1 Open the airway by gently tilting the person's forehead back with one hand and lifting their chin with the other.

2 Check for any signs of breathing. Look for chest movement, or for sounds or heat coming from their mouth.

3 Put them in the recovery position (see page 96).

4 Call the emergency services for help and stay with the person until they arrive, regularly checking to see if their breathing has changed at all while you wait.

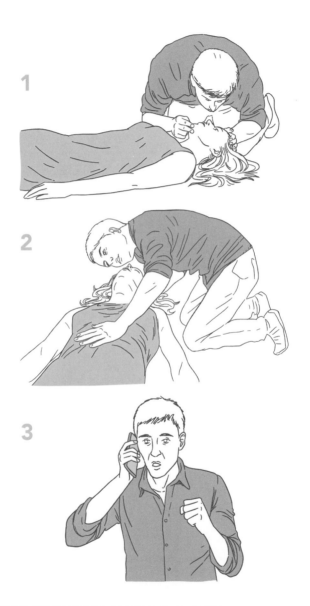

1

2

3

WHAT TO DO IF SOMEONE IS UNRESPONSIVE AND NOT BREATHING

If your fellow student is unresponsive and not breathing, you will have to perform CPR (cardiopulmonary resuscitation): a combination of chest compressions and rescue breaths. But first, call the emergency services.

Chest compressions

1   Kneel beside the person and place the end of your palm towards the end of the breastbone in the centre of their chest.

2   Place your other hand on top of the first and interlock your fingers but stay away from their ribs.

3   With your arms straight lean over the person, pressing down on their breastbone by about 5-6 cm (for an adult).

4   Keeping your hands where they are, release pressure until their chest is in the normal position – this is one compression. Repeat 30 times to the rhythm of the Bee Gees' song 'Stayin' Alive' to help you keep the correct speed. You should achieve 100 to 200 compressions per minute.

Rescue breaths

Once you've done a set of compressions, give the casualty two rescue breaths.

1   Open the casualty's airway, hold their nose closed, take a deep breath and blow the air into the casualty's mouth until their chest rises.

2   Then lift away and let their chest fall. Repeat once more, followed by chest compressions, and continue until help arrives. If they start to breathe normally again, stop CPR and put them in the recovery position.

Put them in the recovery position

You will need to put someone in the recovery position if they have responded positively to the CPR.

1 Kneel down in front of the casualty and place their arm that's nearest to you at a right angle to their body, palm facing upwards.

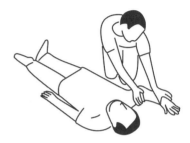

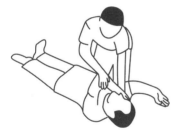

2 Take their arm that's furthest from you and bend it so their hand is positioned on their opposite cheek, palm facing away from the cheek.

3 Lift their leg that's furthest from you so the knee is bent and the foot is flat on the floor. Next, roll them on their side by moving the bent knee across their body to the ground. As they roll over, the hand placed on their cheek should become a support for their head.

4 Gently tilt their head back to ensure their airway is open. Phone the emergency services and keep checking the casualty's breathing until they arrive.

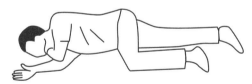

How to apply a dressing

1   First, wash the wound and make sure there's no dirt or grit in it.

2   For small cuts, just use a plaster. For anything bigger, use a sterile pad with medical tape.

3   Cut the sterile pad so that it covers the whole of the wound with a little extra to make sure the surrounding area is covered.

4   Place the pad on the wound, using surgical gloves if possible. Make sure that nothing touches the part of the pad that will be in direct contact with the wound.

5   Use ample amounts of medical tape to hold the pad in place.

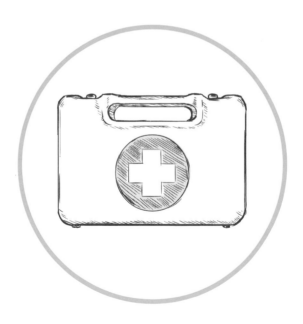

CREATE A FIRST-AID KIT

It's good practice to have a shared first-aid kit in your halls or student house in case of any emergencies. Here is a list of the most common items you should have handy:

- Painkillers
- An assortment of strong fabric plasters – waterproof plasters will slip off the minute you start to sweat
- Blister pads
- Gauze bandages
- Safety pins
- Antiseptic wipes and cream
- Antiseptic/surgical gloves
- Eye-wash
- Burn gel/cream
- Sunscreen (with an SPF of 15 or higher)
- Aftersun cream or lotion

MAINTAIN YOUR HEALTH

Being a student can take a toll on your health, both physically and mentally. Physically, you may notice that you are putting on weight and feeling sluggish due to a higher consumption of fatty foods and alcohol, combined with a decrease in exercise. Mentally, the stress of the exam period or financial worries might make you suffer from insomnia, panic attacks, and/or regular headaches or nausea.

If you feel it's all becoming too much for you, make sure you book an appointment immediately with the relevant student services contact at your university. The student services department usually consists of financial advisers, health and well-being practitioners, counsellors, as well as accommodation, learning difficulty, disability and international student support teams.

HOME, SWEET HOME

In this chapter you will find out how to:

- Choose a houseshare
- Create a cleaning rota
- Clean appliances
- Do the laundry
- Recycle
- Make simple repairs

CHOOSE YOUR HOUSEMATES

It's never easy knowing how many, and what type, of people you should share a house with. There is no formula for perfect (student) living conditions, which makes it very difficult when you have to make the big decision of who to live with once you move out of halls.

You may think that sharing a house with fun, crazy peers will offer you the best student experience there is, but having party animals around you 24/7 may be exhausting – and could lead to friction between you and your housemates. Equally, you may think you would like the easy life and opt for living with someone who is chilled out – however, if they trump you at being laid-back, you might start to think they are just plain lazy.

This isn't scientifically proven by any means, but it's often said that sharing with a group of people who each bring something different to the table is the best formula for harmonious living. For example, a successful houseshare usually has one alpha personality, who will tend to slot into the role of organiser and delegator (two strong-minded people battling it out all the time could lead to a house constantly filled with disagreements). To balance out the big personality, it's often wise to have someone who is a good listener and can calm situations down, if things get heated. Then there is the logical thinker who will put ideas forward in a clear and concise manner, if ever the group feels that the alpha is being pushy about something the majority doesn't agree with. Lastly, there's the social butterfly who acts as the glue of the group and keeps everyone in a positive mood. Of course, finding your houseshare dream team might not consist of these exact personality types, but it might help you to keep this principle of balancing personalities in mind.

Finally, make sure you stay true to your values. How do you feel about bad hygiene? Can you put up with smokers? Are you happy to live with someone who's a bit of a liability when they're drunk? Consider all of these things, and evaluate what you are able to put up with and what would make you seethe. Unfortunately, there can be occasions where someone who is a good friend socially could be a nightmare to live with – and this could end up putting a strain on your relationship.

ENJOY A NO-DRAMA HOUSESHARE

The most common occurrences of people falling out in a houseshare are usually over the smallest things. Not washing dishes after you've cooked and general lack of tidying up after yourself can be two of the biggest causes of a potential World War Three. Another very touchy subject is using other people's food. Before you do anything that could be deemed as disrespectful or thoughtless, ask yourself how you would like it if it was done to you. Often the answer is, of course, a definite no.

Here are some other scenarios best avoided if you don't want your house to become a part of the *EastEnders* set:

- Playing music too loudly

- Having friends stay without clearing it with your other housemates, especially if it happens frequently

- Hogging the TV remote

- Not paying for communal items, such as washing-up liquid or toilet paper

- Walking into someone's bedroom without knocking

- Borrowing other people's stuff without their permission

- Being a rowdy drunk

If a situation does start to bother you, it is best to nip it in the bud straight away rather than stewing on it, being passive aggressive or bitching about it to your other housemates. Most of the time, the person who has annoyed you will respect you for telling them and will change their ways to create a more peaceful environment. It might be helpful to set up monthly catch-ups as an open forum to discuss any issues. By doing this everyone will be on the same page.

CREATE A FAIR CLEANING ROTA

No student wants to be the one cleaning the house while their housemates laze around and watch TV. Create a cleaning rota as soon as you move in to make sure that the chores are divided up fairly. Everyone can get on board from the start and it will help to create a happy, argument-free environment. This may not go down well with everyone in the house – if everyone but you feels that they are cleaning regularly without the aid of a rota (and if their feeling is correct) then you may have to organise yourself to clean.

First you'll need to get together and have a brainstorm about all the jobs that will need doing around the house on a weekly, fortnightly and monthly basis. List them down on a piece of paper. Next to each chore, add one, two or three stars depending on the difficulty and duration of the task. For example, taking out the bins would be one, but cleaning the bathroom would be three. Make sure you discuss whether you'd like to include daily general upkeep tasks (e.g. washing the dishes or wiping down the surfaces after cooking) *before* you write the rota – to ensure these types of jobs are either factored in or omitted. It's usually preferable to have everyone clean up after themselves and to save the big jobs for the rota.

Transfer the chores onto a whiteboard, if you have one, or onto a spreadsheet (that can be emailed or printed and pinned to the wall for everyone to see). Every month, rotate the jobs so that everyone gets an equal share of the duties. A typical cleaning rota could look like the following example:

Chores	Difficulty	Person responsible	Week 1	Week 2	Week 3	Week 4
Dusting communal areas	**					
Vacuuming/mopping communal area floors	**					
Cleaning fridge/freezer	***			n/a	n/a	n/a
Cleaning bath/shower, bathroom sink and toilet	**					
Cleaning kitchen appliances, e.g. oven, microwave, toaster	***			n/a	n/a	n/a
Deep cleaning of kitchen sink and counters	**			n/a	n/a	n/a
Cleaning mirrors	*					
Taking out rubbish and recycling	*					
Checking smoke detectors	*			n/a	n/a	n/a
Mowing lawn (if applicable)	***			n/a	n/a	n/a

SELECT THE BEST CLEANING PRODUCTS

You can go a really long way with water, soap, baking soda and vinegar. These last two can cut through almost all grease and grime, and are much more cost-effective than constantly buying bottles of branded cleaners. However, it might be worth keeping an antibacterial surface cleaner for the kitchen as you'll be sharing it with lots of people and want to be safe when it comes to making food. In the same way, an antibacterial surface cleaner is also a good idea for the bathroom.

CLEAN YOUR KITCHEN

You should wipe down the surfaces with a clean cloth every day to get rid of any germs from food preparation. Sweep (or vacuum) or mop the floors every couple of days to get rid of any crumbs or dirt.

On a weekly basis, run a cloth over the hob to collect any food debris that has built up during cooking. Use a spray cleaner to cut through the grease and grime that has built up there. Similarly, look under the drying rack and you'll be surprised to see the build-up of sludge and soap on the rack and draining board.

If you have a gas stove, clean the burners of your hob about once a month. These are the metal rings above your oven and they cover the burners, and they can get a bit crusty over time. Soap and water will do just fine.

If anything is spilt in the fridge or freezer, particularly if meat juices, clean it up immediately or you risk food poisoning.

CLEAN AN OVEN

1   If you're cooking something in the oven and it spills over, sprinkle salt over it as soon as you've finished cooking, while the oven is still hot. Leave it for 15 minutes and the spill should have turned to ash.

2   Wait for the oven to cool and then wipe up the ash with a wet cloth.

3   Every month, take out the metal racks and use fine steel wool to scrub them with a mixture of baking soda and lemon juice. Then hose them down outside or leave them to soak in your sink and wipe off the dirt after 10 minutes.

4   Deep clean the inside by putting the lowest rack back in the oven and fill a large, deep baking tray with water and half a cup of white vinegar. Place this on the rack and leave in the oven at 180°C (350°F) until the water-vinegar solution starts bubbling and steaming.

5   Take the tray out of the oven and spray the inside with water-vinegar spray (this should be a different water-vinegar solution to the one you have just used to deep clean the oven). Be careful with this as the oven will still be hot. Close the oven door and let it stand for 30 minutes.

6   Once the oven has cooled enough, give it a good wipe down and it should come up sparkling, or at least very much better than it was before.

CLEAN A MICROWAVE

Don't use any cleaning products on the inside of this, as some of the chemicals might linger when you go to use it after it's been cleaned. Instead fill a microwave-safe mug with boiling water and microwave for two minutes. The water will convert to steam and will allow you to easily scrub off any spills or burnt-on food, but wait a while until it has cooled down.

If your microwave pongs a bit, add some lemon juice to the water before you start microwaving it.

CLEAN A TOILET

Don't just flush and run after you've been. Check the loo to be sure it's in a pleasant condition for the next person. It's considered good manners to leave the loo seat down – and the lid too – particularly after a longer visit! Toilets should be deep cleaned once a week to keep germs and viruses at bay, or more often if there's been a virulent stomach bug in your household. Wear rubber gloves if needed, but keep them for this purpose only.

1   Take the long-handled loo brush, usually found in its holder beside the toilet, and scrub away any stubborn residue or streaks left after flushing.

2   Tap the arm of the brush against the side of the seat to shake off drips before transferring back to its holder.

3   Carefully squirt strong, thick bleach under the inside rim and around the toilet bowl, or use a special-purpose toilet cleaner for the job. (If you want to do your bit for the planet, there are some inexpensive, environmentally friendly products available that do the job just as well.) Leave this on for around 10 minutes to neutralise bacteria while you work on the outside of the toilet (including the flush handle and the area around the seat hinges).

4   Work from the top down to the floor with toilet cleaner and a disposable cloth. Then clean all the seat surfaces, including the lid and the rim underneath the seat.

5 With the loo brush, scrub any stains or limescale marks under the rim and inside the toilet bowl. Tip waste water from the loo brush holder down the loo. Add a little bleach to the bottom of the holder. Then close the toilet lid and flush away the bleach.

6 It's a good idea to wash the handbasin and bathroom door handles at the same time, but using a separate cloth!

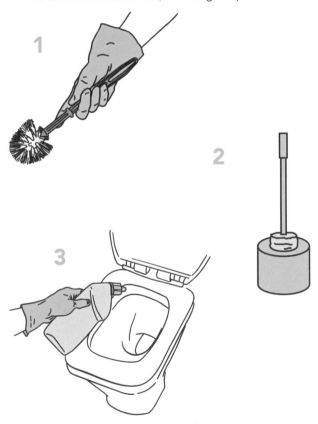

4

5

6

PACK AWAY YOUR BED SHEETS

If you have spare linen sets and they take up a lot of space in your bedroom, there is a way to make them more compact: fold the bed sheet, duvet cover and pillowcases as you usually would, but leave one pillowcase spare. Take the folded sheets and slide them inside the spare pillowcase.

If you have fitted sheets, which are convenient to use but a pain to fold, try this folding method to make life a little easier: place the sheet on a large flat surface with the elasticated side pieces flapped over on top and smooth the material flat. Take one of the short edges to match up with the other one, tucking in any stray side-piece fabric. Repeat this folding action until the sheet is the desired size for storage.

REMOVE STAINS FROM CLOTHES/FURNITURE

UPHOLSTERY

If the fabric is removable and washable, soak the fabric in a bowl of cold water for approximately 30 minutes. Treat with pre-wash stain remover before machine washing according to the fabric type.

For fixed furnishing fabric, blot the stain as much as possible. Mix a small squirt of washing-up liquid with cool water so it's not too soapy and sponge the stain with a clean, white cloth. Blot up all the liquid and repeat the cleaning process until the stain has disappeared. Sponge with cold water to remove any soap and blot dry.

CARPETS

Act quickly when trying to prevent red wine stains! Blot the stain continuously with dry, white paper kitchen towels until you can no longer see any colour on the paper. Press lightly with your shoeless foot on the kitchen towel to help the blotting. However, *don't rub* the stain, as this will set the stain further into the carpet fibres. Add a little water and continue to blot until the stain has lifted. This technique can be employed for any type of liquid carpet stains.

For food stains, gently lift off thick spills and chunky pieces with a blunt knife before attempting to blot. Use diluted washing-up liquid (as directed in the 'Upholstery' section above) or spray with a good carpet stain remover, following the manufacturer's directions. Repeat if necessary. Vacuum once the area has dried.

DO THE LAUNDRY

Wash at high temperatures (60°C or above) to kill bacteria and keep whites brighter, but use the 30°C or 40°C settings for a normal wash. Run the washing machine monthly on empty at 95°C to maintain performance.

Sort your dirty laundry into piles for separate washes:

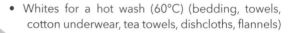

- Whites for a hot wash (60°C) (bedding, towels, cotton underwear, tea towels, dishcloths, flannels)

- Coloured cottons suitable for a hot wash (as above)

- Whites for a warm wash (shirts, T-shirts, skirts, shorts, jeans, trousers)

- Coloureds for a warm/cool wash (as below)

- Delicates for a cool/gentle wash (silk, lace, mesh, synthetic clothing)

- Woollens and silk (jumpers, scarves, gloves): wash these by hand unless you have a handwash/woollens or silk setting on your washing machine

TOP TIPS

- Colours on some items will run if they're not washed at the correct temperature.

- Wash similar colours together (i.e. light colours together, or dark colours together).

- If clothes are only lightly soiled, select the express wash function on your washing machine.

- Because of their absorbent nature, towels need less washing detergent than other items.

- Close zips and link up hooks and eyes so they can't catch on other items.

- Empty the machine as soon as possible after the load has finished to prevent damp clothes from starting to smell musty.

DRYING CLOTHES WITHOUT A TUMBLE DRYER

If hanging clothes outside is not practical, a heated drying rack is a good investment and is very cost-effective. Peg trousers, jeans and skirts at the waistband; shirts, tops and T-shirts should be hung from the shoulders or dried on hangers. Don't overlap clothing as items will take longer to dry. Dry woollens flat to keep their shape.

Machine wash

Machine wash at 30 degrees

Handwash

Bleach

Tumble dry

Tumble dry normal, low heat

Tumble dry normal, high heat

Iron

Iron low heat

Iron high heat

Dry clean

Dry clean, any solvent

Dry clean, petroleum solvent only

Dry clean, any solvent except trichloroethylene

CHANGE A FUSE

Fuses are safety devices that break the electrical current in order to prevent circuits from overheating or catching fire.

If one of the fuses has tripped in your home's fuse box, you simply need to flip the switch (that's facing the wrong way) up or down so it is facing the same way as the other fuse switches.

Fuses are also found in the plugs of electrical devices and appliances. When something electrical doesn't work any more, don't assume it's broken and throw it away – replace the fuse first, as this could be the reason it stopped working. However, if the item blows the fuse again, then take this as a warning: it means there's probably a fault in the device and it should be repaired or replaced.

Standard fuse ratings are 3, 5 or 13 amps. Always replace a fuse with one of the same amp rating. They cost very little to buy in hardware stores, so keep a variety at home for emergencies.

Look for the fuse holder on the reverse side of the plug. Gently prise the plug open using a flat-headed screwdriver. Remove the fuse and replace it. In some older plugs, the back cover must be removed by unscrewing the large screw near the base of the plug to access the fuse. Screw the cover back on when the new fuse is in place.

Fused connection units contain ceramic fuses. Switch off the unit before using the screwdriver to remove the fuse holder, then change the fuse as described above.

CHANGE A LIGHTBULB

Make sure the light switch is off and unscrew or twist slightly to release the light bulb. Take it with you to buy a replacement, paying special attention to the wattage and type of fitting it uses (bayonet, Edison screw cap, spotlights).

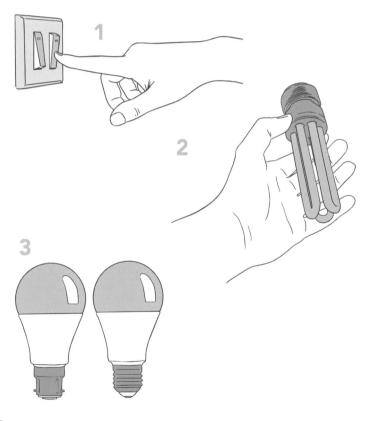

HOW TO
RECYCLE

Plastic and general waste are playing on a lot of people's minds these days as the media increasingly exposes the ways in which we are harming the planet. Do your bit for the environment by recycling more – here's a list of the plastics you can and can't recycle:

1 **PET or PETE (polyethylene terephthalate):** Mainly clear drinks bottles and also some food packaging. Recyclable but not reusable. Instead of buying disposable drinks bottles, why not save your money and the environment by purchasing a reusable bottle or flask?

2 **HDPE (high-density polyethylene):** Bottles used for things such as milk, washing-up liquid and cosmetics. Recyclable and reusable.

3 **PVC (polyvinyl chloride):** Clear food wrapping, shower curtains and toys. Difficult to recycle. Rather than using cling film, why not use recyclable baking paper with elastic bands instead?

4 **LDPE (low-density polyethylene):** Bags to package bread, carrier bags, squeezable bottles and four-/six-pack can holders. Currently difficult to recycle, although plans are in place to try to change this. A number of supermarkets take carrier bags for recycling. Instead of paying extra for 5p or 10p bags each time you go shopping, why not purchase something sturdier that can be reused again and again?

5 **PP (polypropylene):** Cereal bags, bottle tops, margarine tubs, crisp bags and straws. Reusable and occasionally recyclable (e.g. cereal bags and margarine tubs can be recycled).

6 **PS (polystyrene):** Packaging for fragile objects and takeaway cups. Not reusable and currently difficult to recycle, although plans are in place to try to change this. Instead of buying takeout coffees from cafés, why not have your coffee inside the café and enjoy the atmosphere?

7 **Other:** Plastics, such as acrylic glass, nylon, polycarbonate, and items made of a mixture of plastics. Not reusable and difficult to recycle.

You must always clean out the packaging thoroughly before placing it in the recycling bin. If you don't, this could cause a whole vanload of recyclable material to go straight to the landfill, as it won't be accepted into the recycling plant if it is contaminated. From now on, think twice before you put your greasy pizza boxes in the recycling bin.

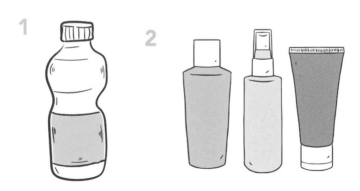

3

4

5

6

7

UNBLOCK A DRAIN

A blocked drain is usually caused by a build-up of matted hair or greasy foods.

1 To unblock it, first try pouring boiling water from the kettle down the plughole.

2 If that doesn't work, try pouring a cup of baking soda followed by a cup of vinegar down the plughole. Don't use that drain for a couple of hours and then pour more boiling water down.

SODA

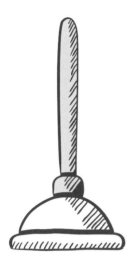

3 If this doesn't work, then unfortunately you'll need to get the contents out with either a plunger or your hands. Use a plunger on the plughole to try to suck up the grossness that lies below.

4 Or uncover the outside drain, don a rubber glove, and search about for the blockage. Hold your nose while you're at it, as this method can bring you into close contact with a very eggy aroma.

BLEED A RADIATOR

The most common cause of faulty heating is a radiator full of air. You'll need to go all Count Dracula and 'bleed' it to fix it. Although this sounds ghoulish and complicated, it is actually quite satisfying and very easy. You'll need a radiator key – which costs less than a pound in most shops.

Turn the heating off. Have a bowl and a towel ready in case the radiator is not full of air and it spurts water all over you. Fit the key over the bolt at the top of your radiator and turn it until you can hear air hissing out. Once it starts to make a bubbling noise, turn the key back to how it was.

FIX A LEAKY PIPE

Most leaky pipes are caused by an aged washer, which is the rubber ring that sits between the pipe and the fitting. You can find cheap replacements at most hardware stores, but always notify your letting agent and check that they're happy for you to proceed with the work.

Turn the water off at the pipe. There should be a water shut-off valve (stopcock) that does this, usually found inside your house near to the road outside. Then turn on the hot and cold taps to drain off the remaining water. Place a bucket under the pipe because when you unscrew it the leftover water will come gushing out. Replace the washer and fit the pipe back into place.

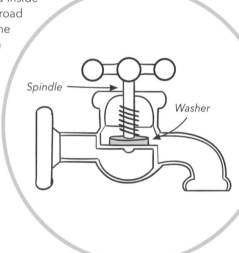

Spindle

Washer

MONEY, MONEY, MONEY

In this chapter you will find out how to:

- Budget
- Save money
- Earn money
- Find discounts

FIND A CHEAP STUDENT HOUSE

You've decided who you are going to live with in your student house – now it's just a matter of finding a house that's great to live in *and* doesn't break the bank. The cheapest student houses often have problems that make them uncomfortable, unhealthy or unsafe to live in – such as damp, mould, weak doors and windows, and faulty electrics! Still, there are some things you can look out for that'll help you save money in the long run.

First, find a house in a location that has good transport links but isn't necessarily central, especially if you will be living in a big city. Check a map app to see how far the house is from a bus stop or train, or if it is connected to the university by a cycle path.

Second, make sure the house you are viewing is well insulated. If it isn't, you could be paying out excessive amounts on heating bills. Check whether the windows are double-glazed, as single-glazed windows are prone to letting the heat out and the cold in!

Third, make sure the taps are in working order and there are no leaks. Also check that the toilet flushes properly – as if it's permanently running water then your water bill will rack up in no time.

Although student houses are in short supply, never put in an offer for the first place you view. It's always worthwhile to make a comparison with others in the same area.

When you place an offer, have a go at haggling. Be polite. The worst that can happen is that the landlord/lady says no. If you have good reason to ask for a reduction in the rent, then this will work in your favour. Give the reason when asking for the reduced rent, but if it is something the landlord/lady can fix, then they might wish to raise the rent once this has been done.

BUDGET

If this is your first time living away from home, then it might well be the first time you've had to think about budgeting. The key is to consider it from the start, as it's all too easy to hide from your finances and not even know how much you have in the bank.

First, set up an online banking account, if you haven't got one already. This allows you to check your balance and all your transactions at the click of a button.

Second, create a spreadsheet with two columns. In the first column write down your total income, such as your maintenance loan and grant, and your monthly salary if applicable. In the same column, list your monthly outgoings – such as 'rent', 'bills', 'food and drink', 'travel and transport', 'clothes and shoes', 'going out', 'toiletries', 'laundry', 'holidays', 'presents', etc. In the second column write down how much you spend on each category, then add them all up and see if you are in minus figures; that is are your outgoings higher than your income? If that's the case, recalculate your average outgoings so that you aren't in the red and *stick to them* to avoid overspending. When deciding where you can cut back, think about the outgoings that are essential and those that are less of a priority. Also consider where you are being wasteful with your money, for example overspending on food or making too many impulse purchases.

There are tons of apps and websites that can help you with your budgeting and keeping track. Here are some to get you started: Pennies (www.getpennies.com), Mint (www.mint.com) and Monzo (https://monzo.com).

CUT BACK ON SPENDING

Sometimes it can seem like your money has nearly all gone before it's even made its way into your bank account. You know you're spending too much, but where are you going wrong? Here are some ideas to help you give up the things that are leaving your wallet empty and bring some positive financial changes to your life:

- Have one no-spend day per week

- Have one party-free week each month

- Rethink the transport you are using to get to uni – public transport offers various money-saving student travel passes

- If you have a car, try to lift-share as much as possible

- Compare energy prices and switch

- Use less water and electricity

- Swap attending the gym with exercise that is free (see pp. 90–92)

- Buddy-up to buy streaming services

- Do your food shop on a full stomach

- Buy in bulk and freeze if necessary

- Make packed lunches and cook meals from scratch

- Buy a reusable water bottle

- Eat more vegetarian meals

- Buy your student-house furniture on the cheap or get it for free from sites such as Gumtree and the Facebook marketplace – it will probably get pretty worn out anyway

- Never take your credit card with you on nights out

- Consider borrowing your study books from the library or buying second-hand wherever possible

FIND DISCOUNTS

It's undisputed that every student loves a discount, but retailers aren't that liberal in dishing them out. So where do you find them?

On enrolling at university, make sure you send off for your student discount card. This will give you the ability to shop at hundreds of shops that offer student discounts and receive up to 20 per cent off the retail price. Most popular high-street shops will advertise this in their shop windows, but, if not, then it's worth asking at the counter – just in case! Otherwise, check which shops offer student discounts by searching online. Being on the ball could save you a lot of money, especially if you're purchasing something expensive.

Download discount apps such as VoucherCodes and VoucherCloud for all sorts of savings, varying from days out to gadgets. These are especially good for birthday ideas, as they will often show activities and restaurants in your area that you've never heard of before – and you'll be able to gift something unusual at a low cost to yourself.

You may have heard of cashback websites, but do you know what they are and how they work? It's quite simple. A cashback website will offer you cashback for different retailers if you make a purchase after clicking from the cashback website page to the retailer's page. The retailer gives the cashback company a commission and part of that goes to you, the buyer. All you have to do is register and then you can take advantage of the discounts – they are small but they all add up!

SAVE MONEY

The problem with money is that it's very difficult to earn, yet very easy to spend! If you're not careful, you'll find that as soon as pay day comes around you'll blow it all on one night out. Why not see if you can become saving-savvy with these money-saving tips?

TOP TIPS

At those times of the year when you receive gift money, e.g. your birthday or Christmas, put it away in a savings account rather than spending it on something you probably don't need.

Try the 365-day, 1p-accumulator challenge – all you need for this is a jar and some pennies! On day one, put one penny in the jar, then on day two put two pennies in the jar and so on and so forth. So that you can live comfortably while saving, restart to 1p at the beginning of each month. At the end of the 365 days, you'll have over £62 saved.

Stop the urge to impulse buy by patiently considering the purchase for 30 days and then re-evaluating whether you really want it. On first seeing the item, write down its name, the price and the date on a piece of paper and stick it to your fridge (and add to your bookmarks if online). When 30 days are up, see how you feel about the item – if you still want it (and can still afford it), then you can buy it! But if you don't want it any more then you'll feel pretty pleased to know that your money hadn't been wasted on something you wouldn't use or wear.

If you can see and access all the money in your current account, it's more likely you'll spend it. Use online banking tools to transfer at least some of your money to a savings account quickly and safely. If you're confident that you won't need to access the money you are putting into a savings account until much later, think about opening up a fixed rate savings account that you can't touch for a certain length of time - or even just a separate account that perhaps offers a better rate of interest for a fixed notice period.

FIND A PART-TIME JOB

Often your student loan won't get you as far as you want it to and you'll need a part-time job for buying those little extras. Not only will a part-time job mean that you have more money, it will also give a good example of how your ability to juggle responsibilities for your CV. It might feel a bit daunting to start looking for work in a new, unfamiliar place, so here are some tips to get you started.

TOP TIPS

Look on the student union web page for vacancies on campus: Jobs will usually be within the bar and catering sectors, although occasionally jobs more relevant to your area of study may come up. You want to snap these opportunities up quickly, as they are the perfect addition to your future CV when you start looking for full-time work after finishing your studies. One benefit of working for your university is that they are likely to be more understanding about your workload and so more flexible with hours than outside companies.

Go to your university's careers service: Book an appointment with them as soon as you have settled in. They will offer you advice on where to look, as well as give you tips on how to smarten up your CV. Most universities have a jobs portal that advertises local part-time vacancies, some of which are exclusive to students. They can also help you to search for a job that is linked to what you want to do after university.

Look for jobs in the run-up to the Christmas period: From September each year, a lot of retailers, restaurants and bars begin to advertise temp jobs that usually end on Christmas Eve or after New Year's Eve. This is the perfect time to secure a position – and if you make a good impression, they might offer you an opportunity to extend your contract or even become permanent.

EARN MONEY WHILE STUDYING

The best way to earn a big chunk of money while studying is by bagging a part-time job (see page 135). However, if you want to earn a little extra cash here and there, alongside your job, here are some ideas to earn you some extra pocket money:

- Become a mystery shopper – you can do this by applying online

- Be self-employed as a food courier

- If you are a creative, self-publish or sell on Etsy

- Enter online competitions – but don't expect to win if you only enter a few; you'll need to put in quite a lot of legwork. To begin with, find competitions by entering the hashtag #competition or #win on Twitter or Instagram

- Be a film extra: all you need to do is register with some extras agencies

- Babysit or dog walk/dog-sit

FIND CHEAP TRAVEL AND ACCOMMODATION WHEN BOOKING A HOLIDAY

After all that exam and assignment stress, it's likely that what you'll really want to do is take a break somewhere abroad. The only problem is that you've spent most of your student loan and need a bargain. Try the following tips to help you get the best deal out there:

- Sign up to an airline's mailing list to generate useful emails that detail special offers and bonus air-mile promotions.

- Book flights in the first four months of the year – and at least 47-53 days before you wish to depart – to get the cheapest price.

- Book with airlines that provide flexible fares, so that you can reserve a seat on your chosen date *and* be able to change that date later, should you need to. This means that you can book off-peak dates and, as long as they're available, fly on peak dates. This is especially useful in a school summer holiday scenario. Some companies will offer free hold luggage and early boarding with this option too, but offers vary so be sure to read the terms and conditions.

- Buy two low-priced one-way tickets as this can be cheaper than a round-trip ticket, so *check* before you buy. The same can also apply to train journeys!

SAVE MONEY ON TOILETRIES

Toiletries can cause a massive dent in your wallet. They all seem to run out at the same time too! Try to be mindful about how much you spend on them and what you buy, as, if you're careful, you can save a wodge of money in the long run.

TOP TIPS

Think about whether brands are worth the extra: A lot of the time, branded products actually contain almost the same ingredients as the non-branded, cheaper products. They only cost more because of their established name and the packaging they come in. When you are next shopping for your toiletries, look at the ingredients on the back of two similar items that have a big price difference and you might be surprised to find that they differ by only one or two ingredients. This is especially true of medicines, such as paracetamol, where the cost of the branded product can be as much as £2 more expensive.

Think about what you actually need: Most of the time we intend to buy essentials, but then get distracted by an array of products that claim to be 'miracle workers'. Don't fall into this marketing trap, as you'll only be disappointed when you find out that the product *doesn't* do what it says on the tin.

Try making your own skincare and haircare products: Google 'DIY skincare recipes' or 'DIY haircare recipes' and you'll discover a whole host of websites that explain how to make your own at a fraction of the cost you would pay in a shop. Chip in with your housemates on buying the bulk ingredients and spend a day making up some of the products.

WORK HARD, PLAY HARDER

In this chapter you will find out how to:

- Play uni drinking games
- Fashion fancy-dress costumes
- Be safe on nights out
- Throw a house party (and clean up after it)
- Save money and socialise
- Find a love interest

HAVE A GOOD FRESHER'S WEEK

This is by far the booziest week of the academic year. The key to surviving it is to pace yourself. But that doesn't mean you can't have fun! If you want to break the ice with your new housemates/people in your dorm, try playing these simple drinking games.

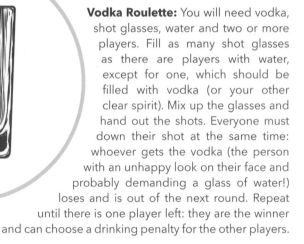

Vodka Roulette: You will need vodka, shot glasses, water and two or more players. Fill as many shot glasses as there are players with water, except for one, which should be filled with vodka (or your other clear spirit). Mix up the glasses and hand out the shots. Everyone must down their shot at the same time: whoever gets the vodka (the person with an unhappy look on their face and probably demanding a glass of water!) loses and is out of the next round. Repeat until there is one player left: they are the winner and can choose a drinking penalty for the other players.

Fifty-Fifty: You will need a beer mat and three or more players for this game. The first player takes the beer mat and flips it into the air; if it lands face up, they nominate another player to drink whatever penalty drink has been decided; if it lands face down, then player who flipped the mat has to down the penalty drink. Each person takes it in turns to flip the mat, with a fifty-fifty chance of either having to drink or nominate someone else.

Sixes: You will need two dice and two or more players. This game is simple but effective if you have a large amount of alcohol to work your way through. Players take it in turns to roll the dice; if the numbers add up to six (for example, a four and a two) or one of them is a six, the player must drink one finger. If a player rolls a double, they must drink fingers equivalent to the number on one of the die – so if they roll a double four, they must drink four fingers. For a double three or double six, both rules apply: a finger for adding up to six, and a number of fingers for the double. So a double six means eight fingers: two for two sixes, plus another six for rolling a double six!

Underwater Karaoke: You will need three or more players. Each player takes it in turn to perform a song for their 'audience'. The catch is that songs cannot be sung – they must be gargled through alcoholic beverages! The other players take turns to identify the song being 'sung', and each incorrect guess is punished by a drinking penalty. If, after a second gargled rendition, none of the players can guess the tune, the performer must finish their drink. Continue for as many rounds as your ears can bear!

PICK A FANCY-DRESS OUTFIT

There are many fancy-dress options you'll be introduced to when you start university, but here's a small selection of the most popular to kick-start your preparations.

RAVE

The 'rave' really doesn't go out of style – after all, who wouldn't want all the fun of a rave combined with the convenience of being at a club or house? Rave-style is super easy to do, and is very easy to adapt, depending on your personal style.

If you want to go old-school, all you need is a cheap, baggy T-shirt, a bucket hat and a whistle hung around your neck. These will all be available cheaply online, or else you can have some fun combing the charity shops for them. A tie-dye or smiley-face T-shirt will really evoke the old rave-in-a-field days of the 1990s. Ideally, get a plastic whistle, or an LED light-up whistle – you're aiming for 'sick rave' rather than 'sports day'.

Buy some UV fluorescent body paints and go to town on your face and arms (and other areas if they're on display!). A stylish swirl of dots about the eyes and brow is a good starting design, but you can do as much or as little as you like.

Girls, if you're looking for a more modern rave costume, a neon tutu-and-bikini-top combo can look really great. If you're going all-out for this, buy some cheap furry material from the local fabric shop and sew it onto fingerless gloves or leg warmers to complete the look. *Guys*, it's harder to cheat your modern rave look, but a neon sleeveless top and some jazzy shades can start you off. If you have the budget, consider stretching to some baggy trousers that you can hang lots of dangly neon and LED accessories from.

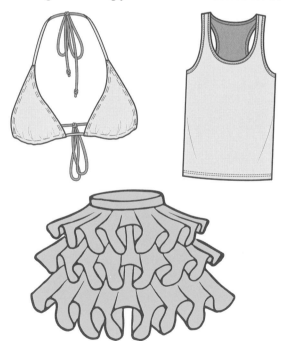

TOGA

No prizes for guessing the costume you need for this one! Here are some simple steps you can follow to create a toga:

1   Pick a plain bed sheet (preferably for a single bed so it doesn't swamp you!). Hold one of the corners with your left hand; leave around 15-20cm between the tip of the corner and your grip so you have something to pin later. Bring it to your left shoulder.

2   Drape the sheet across your chest and tuck it under your right arm so it fits snugly against your chest.

3   The sheet will ideally be knee length. If you notice the sheet is too long, fold it until it is the correct length and secure with safety pins.

4   With your right hand wrap the sheet around your back and tuck it under your left arm. Then wrap it around the front of your chest again, repeating until there isn't much more material left.

5   Now bring the second corner up over your back so it meets with the first end. Secure them together with a brooch, pin or simple knot.

6   Fix the layers tightly with safety pins. Do a wiggle and a jiggle to make sure that the toga won't fall off and isn't uncomfortable.

7   Top off the look with a gold belt (or gold material), some sandals and a bunch of grapes.

8   Provided you don't spill red wine over your newly created toga, you can wash it later so it can go back on your bed.

SCHOOL DISCO

There's guaranteed to be a geeky school disco at some point in your university life – probably within the first week, actually! Here are some tips on how to look the part without spending too much:

- **School shirt or polo top:** Some people can still fit into their old school uniform (you will get bonus points for authenticity), but if you don't have one to hand (or one that fits), you can always buy a small pack of them without it costing too much, especially if you share the pack with other people who need one.

- **Black or grey trousers, shorts or skirt:** You are bound to have some trousers lying around at home, so make sure that you take them with you. If you want to step it up a gear, then grey shorts with ankle-length white socks will attract a few looks.

- **Eyeliner pencil:** This will come in handy for drawing on freckles. If you have a polo shirt, you can also use the pen to get other people to write things on it. It's fun to take the pen out with you and see how many randomers you can persuade to write on you or your shirt (it often ends up being you!). The next morning you are bound to find some obscure messages!

- **Thick-rimmed glasses:** If you don't have any of these, use a pair of 3D glasses and remove the plastic bits.

- **The school tie:** If you don't have a tie, and neither do friends or family (ask those who are younger than you), then you can pick one up from a fancy-dress shop for a couple of quid.

BEACH/HAWAIIAN

This fancy-dress theme often happens in the depths of winter, so don't forget to put a coat on over your scant outfit. Here are some beach party ideas:

- For *girls*, a grass skirt is always a good investment (*guys*, no reason why you wouldn't look good in one either!). If you don't fancy wearing a bikini or making your own coconut shell bra, then a brightly coloured top will more than suffice.

- *Guys* – you could wear some flowery shorts or, if you want to be really daring, try squeezing into your teeny, tiny trunks. If you don't feel comfortable baring your chest, and you feel that flower-on-flower is a bit OTT, then buy a cheap, flesh-coloured T-shirt and draw some pecs and abs on it for that elusive 'beach bod'.

- Flip-flops, a straw hat, sunglasses, garlands and a good old inflatable rubber ring or beach ball are all accessories that will add to the effect.

'WHERE'S WALLY?'

This idea is perfect for a student night out as it's cheap and the main point is to appear the same as your friends so there'll be no rivalry of who looks best.

For guys and girls, all you need is a red-and-white stripy top, some thick-rimmed glasses. and a red-and-white hat with a bobble attached to it. It might be worth buying it all together if you can find sets of the clothing as it will probably work out cheaper.

If you have a fear of looking the same as everyone else, you can always dress up as the wizard or the robber.

PACE YOURSELF

It's so easy to get overexcited during freshers' week, or at any point in your busy student social life, that most people will claim to have experienced one night they regret. To avoid being the talk of the town, take heed of the following advice:

1 Don't drink on an empty stomach as the alcohol will go to your head more quickly – and with more force. Eating before drinking can slow the absorption of alcohol by your body, but remember: it won't actually stop you from getting drunk.

2 For every alcoholic drink you consume, have a glass of water. It's the simplest way to keep yourself hydrated and lessen the severity of your hangover.

3 Drink something that *tastes* like alcohol. This sounds weird, but it works. If you order drinks that taste distinctly alcoholic, such as wine or beer, it should take you longer to finish than something sweeter, such as a spirit with a mixer or an alcopop.

4 This might seem like common sense, but choose a beverage that contains less alcohol. Bear in mind that one can of regular beer is about 5 per cent alcohol, one glass of wine is approximately 12 per cent alcohol, and one shot of spirit is about 40 per cent alcohol. And when it comes to spirits, research suggests that drinking clear spirits will give you less of a hangover than if you drink dark spirits. This is due to the quantity of the congeners – chemicals that contribute to the taste and aroma of the alcohol – in the drinks, which are thought to have an effect on hangover symptoms.

5 Stick to the same type of drink all night rather than mixing them – and be incredibly careful if you're drinking cocktails, as it's not immediately obvious how many shots of alcohol they contain.

4

5

BE SAFE ON A NIGHT OUT

You'll probably have some of the best nights of your life when you are at uni, but always be aware of your surroundings and the people in them, including the route to and from your venue, as there'll be no security around to help you out in times of trouble. Here are some top tips to help you stay safe:

1   Avoid putting yourself in a position of vulnerability by staying with your friends at all times, or at least being aware of their whereabouts. It's best to swap phone numbers with more than just one of the people you are out with, even if you don't know them well. This gives you a Plan B in case you have any communication issues and can't find them.

2   Limit the amount of money you take out with you. Set yourself a budget and take that out in cash, leaving your card behind at home. Not only will this make your generous, drunken self think twice about buying everyone drinks, it will also help you stay inconspicuous to thieves. As soon as you start flashing all of that student loan money (that technically isn't yours) you could become the perfect target to steal from.

3   Make sure that your drink is always in your hand or in your view, such as on the table you're sitting at. Reported incidents of drink-spiking are on the rise. Most criminals will resort to spiking people's drinks because it makes it easier to steal their valuables and/or sexually assault them. Symptoms will usually kick in after 30 minutes and consist of nausea and vomiting, hallucinations, paranoia, disorientation, blurred vision, loss of balance, blackouts, and difficulty in concentrating or speaking. The most severe symptom is unconsciousness. If you notice any of these symptoms, whether in yourself or in a friend, tell

someone you trust immediately (such as one of the friends you went out with) so they can help you and watch out for your safety. Report it to the police as soon as possible.

4 Another technique criminals use to spike drinks is to offer the victim one. Whether you're having a quiet night at your local or a wild night out at a club, if you get chatting to someone and they ask if you'd like a drink, *be careful*. It's fine to accept the offer, but make sure you go with them to the bar and watch your drink all the time until it is in your hand. And then guard it carefully!

5 If you're going to walk back after a night out, make sure you're with friends and that you only have a short distance to go. Keep to roads that are well lit and avoid parks and alleyways, even if it does take you a little longer. If in doubt, always call a cab or book an Uber, as it's better to spend your precious money getting home safely than to risk your life.

6 If you live in a bustling city, there's bound to be some sort of public transport available to you if you don't want to splash out on a taxi. However, always be alert to the people in your vicinity, as trouble is most likely to start between people when they've been drinking. If someone nearby seems rowdy, discreetly move seats so you are further away. If you're on your own with them, go to the next carriage of the train or the bottom deck of the bus where there are other people around.

CURE A HANGOVER

There are so many red herrings when it comes to knowing what cures a hangover, but the advice below should help you feel slightly more human:

1   Studies suggest that honey is good for hangovers because it contains fructose, which helps speed up the breakdown of alcohol. Lemon is said to help the recovery time as it has alkalising properties, which help rebalance pH levels in the body. So while you're having a pint of water the day after, try adding some honey or a slice of lemon to it.

2   Sleeping when it's specifically daytime won't help cure a hangover, but sleeping as much as possible the next day will help make you feel better. Although we tend to 'crash' when we've had too much to drink, our actual sleep is disrupted by our body's attempt at breaking down the alcohol. You are permitted to have as many power naps the next day as you like!

3   Exercise is good for a hangover if taken in moderation and at the right time. As your body will feel fragile, don't go setting your alarm for 7 a.m. to get in that early morning 10K, but, if you have the motivation, try going for a brisk walk or a leisurely bike ride (as long as you're not still over the limit) after lots of water and some food. The fresh air will work wonders for you.

4   Adopt 'rehydrate don't dehydrate' as your motto for the night *and* the morning after. Many of the symptoms of a hangover are simply symptoms of dehydration. Drink one glass of tap water for every two alcoholic beverages you enjoy on the night (as a bonus - it's free!). The next day keep that cool, sweet (don't forget the honey!) water flowing and include some hydrating snacks as well. Fruits such as watermelon and papaya are not only full of refreshing water, but also have a high sugar, salt and mineral content, which will all lend a healing hand to the hungover student.

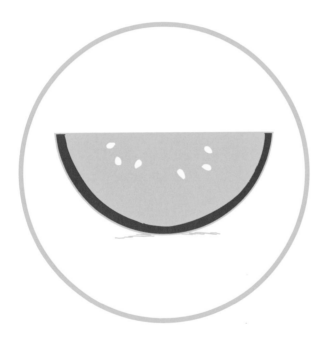

THROW A HOUSE PARTY

It feels great organising and hosting a party, held in your house, that your guests love, but it can also be quite stressful. A bit of preparation can help alleviate your stress and worry, so try to get everything you need in place before the day of the party. Also, make sure that you have agreement from your housemates before you start inviting a horde of people. If you are stuck for ideas, here are some suggestions:

1920S SPEAKEASY-STYLE COCKTAIL PARTY

Invite your guests to come as gangsters, molls and flappers, and get ready for a wild evening of jazz, canapés and cocktails.

1970S DISCO FEVER

Dust down the glitter ball, grab a copy of *Saturday Night Fever* and get your guests to don their flares! There are some great 1970s-inspired cocktails and snacks you could serve too – cheese and pineapple on sticks, cocktail sausages, olives, or, if you want to push the boat out, how about a fondue?

1980S COCKTAIL NIGHT

Channel your inner Tom Cruise with a 1980s-inspired cocktail party. Ask your guests to come in leg warmers and play popular 1980s tunes, perhaps some Wham!. Set up a 'Big Hair Blowout Bar' with hairdryers, brushes and plenty of hairspray, so you can have fun experimenting with different whacky hairdos. Don't forget the glow-stick bracelets for your guests, and you can even decorate the room with glow-stick balloons – just blow up a balloon, pop a glow stick inside it, tie it up, and *voilà!*

EUROVISION PARTY

Of course this only happens once a year, but make sure the date is in your calendar as it's the perfect chance to host a party that'll have everyone singing (badly) and laughing hysterically. Get each guest to pick a country to represent and ask them to bring a dish that the country is famous for, as well as to dress up in the colours of its flag. If you fancy making it a night of drinking, you'll be able to find tons of drinking-game rules on the internet.

CRAFT COCKTAIL NIGHT

If you want something a little more sedate from your evening, then invite your more creative friends around for an evening of making, shaking and mixing.

A craft cocktail is one where every element is tailored specifically to the drink. You can serve them in custom glassware, poured over bespoke ice cubes, and mixed with delicious home-made syrups.

Get yourself a whole assortment of glasses, spirits, liqueurs, syrups, fruits and herbs – and have fun mixing some unique craft cocktails, as well as coming up with inventive names for them!

'LET'S FLAMINGLE'

This tropical theme is perfect for a summer cocktail party, and there are plenty of party accessories available to really make the most of the theme – such as piñatas, inflatable palm trees, flamingoes, beach balls, a mini paddling pool (perhaps filled with ice to serve as a drinks cooler), buckets and spades (for snacks and nibbles), beach towels draped over the chairs, or deck chairs if you have them, and paper umbrellas (for your drinks). Life's a beach!

MASSIVE (HOUSE) PARTY

Even if you don't want to throw a themed party, there are a few things you can do to jazz up your house and get it party-ready. Choose several rooms to be the party rooms and several rooms to be 'furniture rooms' and move all the knick-knacks and furniture (except chairs) from the party rooms to the furniture rooms. Lock the furniture rooms so no one can access them. Buy coloured bulbs and replace the plain bulbs in the designated party rooms with them. Tape shut any cupboards or fridges that you don't want accessed. Students nab the strangest things and you don't want your yoghurt or your saucepans to go missing. Keep a couple of rolls of toilet paper in one of the locked rooms so you can refill the toilets when they run out.

TIDY UP AFTER A PARTY

1 If your housemates approved your party, let them know in advance that you will tidy everything up and they really needn't worry. During the party, it's recommended to clean as you go, as much as possible, but this is easier said than done! Clean up spills and breakages as soon as they happen.

2 If you wake up and your hangover is too much to bear, without even checking the state of your house, then take one step at a time. The first step is to try to sleep it off for a little longer. Trying to create tidiness with a befuddled head may lead to scenes of emotional turmoil.

3 The best way to tackle a post-party tidy-up is methodically. To begin, gather all the cups, bottles and glasses in the kitchen and sort them into piles for washing-up and recycling. Once these have been washed, dried and put away, begin collecting all the plates and serving dishes and repeat the process.

4 Then get a black bag and put any rubbish you see lying around into it. Separate out the recycling and place it in the appropriate bin, making sure it's clean first.

5 Finally, give the area in which you were gathered a quick hoover and dust, and clean the bathroom and toilet. Check any electrical or valuable items to make sure they are still working – or haven't been inadvertently taken – and pick up the cigarette ends from the garden and outside areas if any smokers attended.

TAKE A BREAK FROM PARTYING

Whether you are trying to save money or just want a pause from student nightlife, there are many ways to occupy yourself without depending on alcohol:

- **Camping:** See if your friends are interested and if so, then you could all chip in some money to buy a tent. A basic one will do, and buying it second-hand is often cheaper. Research a camping spot – if you want to wild camp make sure it is legal in the country in which you are living before you set off – and see what your travel options are. Go by car if you have access to one. Remember that you could possibly hire a car or use public transport, although this may be trickier to arrange.

- **Board-game night:** Have a good old-fashioned get-together with your friends and host an evening of board games. Tell each guest to bring a board game and a snack to share with the group. Time will fly as you battle it out to decide who the ultimate board-game champion will be.

- **Poker night:** A poker night is a great way to socialise with friends, as long as you all know what you are doing. You can place bets, even if it's just for sweets or chocolates, as this will add an extra element of excitement to your evening.

- **Film night:** At least one person in your group of friends will have a subscription to a TV- and film-streaming service. Move all the duvets downstairs and set up a comfy area where you can sprawl out. If you want a super-cheap night in, buy some supermarket pizzas in advance or order a takeaway delivery if you have money to spare.

- **Go for an evening walk/bike ride:** There's nothing like being outside lapping up the fresh air, especially if you have spent the day indoors attending lectures or studying. The exercise will also do wonders for any stress or anxiety you might be feeling. If you are based in a city and you want a change of scenery, look for some suitable rural places nearby. Make sure you give yourself plenty of time to get there and back before it starts to get dark – the best time of year to explore is in the summer months.

- **Attend the theatre, or a talk or a comedy night:** A night out is relatively expensive, so why not spend the same amount of money on seeing a play or a comedy show, or perhaps a talk about a topic that interests you? If no one else is interested in going with you, this is the perfect excuse to have some alone time.

- **Nothing:** Sometimes the best way to escape it all and relax is to do absolutely nothing. Pencil in an evening each week or month to play some soothing music, diffuse essential oils in your room, and lie down on your bed, eyes closed, in peace.

MAKE THE MOST OF FREE TIME

As you become more familiar with your study timetable, you'll notice there are certain days that are less busy than others. This is when you can start introducing extra activities into your schedule. It's good to do this gradually, one at a time – so you know exactly where your limits are before you overload yourself. If you had any sports or hobbies back home that you'd like to continue, check if your university does them before you look elsewhere. If it's a popular sport, it's likely that it will, and you will, get the chance to enter regional leagues and competitions. This is a fantastic way to meet new like-minded people.

If you aren't into sports, then find out what sorts of societies you can join. Most institutions have an array of clubs to choose from. Many of them encourage newcomers, while some societies only accept students who are already at a certain level or have a good knowledge of the subject. As long as the club accepts fresh-faced applicants, there's no shame in joining the Harry Potter Society in order to learn more about this topic!

If you have no interest in the societies available, but you do have a burning passion to pursue a topic close to your heart, you can always start a new society. You'll need to contact your student union to find out how you can apply. There'll be a lot of legwork involved, but you'll feel a great sense of achievement once it's up and running. Plus, it'll look great on your CV.

GET A DATE

It's often the case that when one of your friends finds a partner, the rest of them follow in quick succession, and they lock themselves away, surfacing only when they break up. For the times when you fancy exploring the world of dating, but don't know where to start, here are a few tips on where you can find love (or just have a bit of fun):

- **Dating apps:** There's a dating app for everyone, everywhere. As you start to become familiar with your university, you'll probably start to recognise the people you swiped right/left for.

- **Clubs or societies:** Join a club or society that you're interested in and the likelihood is that you'll meet people who interest you, and some who you might even find romantically attractive.

- **In your class:** You'll spend a lot of time with those who are studying the same subject as you. Naturally you'll probably build relationships with classmates who are similar to you, but, between study chatter, you might find that you have a deeper connection with someone a little different.

HOW TO

ORGANISE A FIRST DATE

Choosing a first date can be tricky. You don't know much about the other person, but it would be good to show your imaginative side by going somewhere other than the cinema. Here are some ideas based on different personality types:

TOP TIPS

- **Sports lovers:** As it's a first date, don't agree to anything too energetic, as you probably don't want them to see you all sweaty (there's always time for that later on!). Instead, why not go on a bike ride, or for a walk, and stop off at a country pub for a bite to eat? Or you could challenge them to a game of crazy golf or ten-pin bowling if you're competitive – but make sure you don't show them that you're a sore loser just yet!

- **Thrill-seekers:** Test your nerves and find out who is the biggest daredevil by going to a theme park. If there isn't a theme park nearby, or you don't have the money to go, check if there are any funfairs locally, as they usually have free entry and you only pay for the rides you want to go on.

- **Geeks:** Find yourself in book heaven by visiting a famous library or go to a museum you haven't been to before. Finish off the day with a coffee in the establishment's café as you discuss the joy of culture.

- **Hopeless romantics:** If you can't stop yourself from creating a fairy-tale vision of your first date in your head, then why not plan a toned-down, but still romantic, picnic? Take a blanket, some fizz, strawberries and other picnic snacks, and enjoy the simplicity of taking in your surroundings and being in good company.

GETTING A REAL JOB

In this chapter you will find out how to:

- Pursue your chosen career path
- Be more employable
- Find work experience opportunities
- Write a CV
- Be interview-ready

RESEARCH YOUR CAREER OPTIONS

Book a careers appointment to discuss job options during your first year. They will be able to offer information on a whole host of jobs that you might not have even considered or known about before. They can also provide details on job requirements and what preliminary work will help you to boost your chances of getting the position you want. A lot of careers require their entry-level employees to have completed work experience or even a work placement. Your first- and second-year summer holidays are the perfect time to complete those, which is why it's good to talk to your careers adviser as soon as possible.

Prospects.ac.uk is a great website to browse your options. It is crammed with information about all types of job options relevant to the subject you studied at college/university, what they entail, what skills and work experience you need for them, and typical employers who recruit graduates. If all this information is a bit overwhelming, they also have a careers quiz, which can help you match your skills and personality to the perfect job.

PURSUE YOUR CAREER PATH

You might think you don't need to start worrying about career options and the best way to secure the job of your dreams until the final year, but this is where many people go wrong. Indeed, between writing your dissertation, studying for exams and writing more essays, you won't have the time to do lots of paid work or volunteering. To help you aim towards a goal, set yourself a yearly plan with targets that you need to have completed by the end of each academic year.

The careers and employability department at your university will be able to help you devise this plan, as well as give you professional advice, so book at least one appointment with them during each academic year. At most academic institutions, you will have the option to use their career services after you've completed your course as well. This can be available to you up to a year after completion, sometimes longer.

So, if you're struggling to write stand-out job applications, or if you think your interview techniques need to be improved, this is the perfect opportunity to introduce yourself to the team – in order to hone your skills and bag a job you are proud of.

PICK THE RIGHT EMPLOYABILITY ACTIVITIES IN YOUR FIRST YEAR

Go to a careers fair in year one. Even if you aren't sure what you want to do, it might give you some inspiration. Make sure you engage with some of the employers in order to get the most out of your attendance. Before you attend, create a list of questions to help prompt you when you are speaking to the employers.

Then follow up on any leads you were able to make at the careers fair. If you managed to get a business card from an employer at one of the stands, check out their website, research the company, and, if you like what they do and think it's relevant to you, email them your interest in taking part in some work experience.

Do at least one week's worth of voluntary work by the end of year one. Depending on the company's flexibility, you might have to do a week straight or you might be able to work one day a week for five weeks. It's always good to stay in contact with the companies you establish relationships with as they can give you a good reference, and might even offer you a job after you graduate.

PICK THE RIGHT EMPLOYABILITY ACTIVITIES IN YOUR SECOND YEAR

Try to decide by year two whether you want to continue studying or go straight into employment after university. Then start researching any particular requirements you need to be aware of – do you need to apply well in advance, are there minimum grades required, or are you required to have a certain amount of work experience? Make sure you know all this information well in advance.

Book another careers appointment at the beginning of year two and set up regular meetings so that you can chart your career- or study-seeking progress.

Plan to do more voluntary work in year two. Try to find new companies to broaden your skill set and opportunities. For example, if you found work with a big company during your first year, arrange to spend some time in a small or independent company in your second. There's often a lot of appeal in working for a big name company in your desired field, but you might find that you prefer the day-to-day life of working in a smaller company. That's what work experience is all about – getting a taste of working life so that you can decide what you really want to do when you graduate!

PICK THE RIGHT EMPLOYABILITY ACTIVITIES IN YOUR FINAL YEAR

In your final year, reduce the hours you put into extracurricular work and focus on your studies, as this is the most important year. However, if you want to carry on with further study, you will need to submit your application form at some point in the year. Speak to an academic adviser and your careers team about this at the very beginning of your final year to plan how long it will take to write and what needs to be included.

FIND WORK EXPERIENCE OPPORTUNITIES

There are various types of work experience opportunities for you to take part in while studying. Some are better suited to take up when you are studying and others are better for when you are on your summer break.

INTERNSHIPS

These are better done during the holidays – so that you can focus all of your attention on gaining skills and experience. If one of your days as an intern conflicts with an academic event, let the employer know before you start. This won't be a poor reflection on you and they should understand that your studies come first.

You should be paid at least the minimum wage. Any internships that you complete can be added to your CV and make sure you ask the employer if they would be happy to provide a reference if needed.

To look for internships, research companies in your local area and check their websites to see if they run internship programmes. The government-run Graduate Talent Pool is an internship database specifically designed for recent graduates who are looking for work experience. You can always speak to a careers adviser too, as they will have a wealth of information about which companies in the area run internship schemes. If you're looking to do your internship further afield, you might want to check out the following websites: absoluteinternship.com, www.city-internships.com, www.crccasia.com and www.theinterngroup.com.

WORK PLACEMENTS

These are sometimes a compulsory part of your course, depending on what you are studying, but can also be arranged independently. The length of the placement varies from one week to a month, and can consist of five working days a week, one working day a week or anything in between. If your application is successful, you will be able to discuss and arrange with the employer a working pattern that is suitable for you. If you are doing a placement that only lasts one week, there's no obligation for the company to pay you, but any placement that runs for a substantial period of time should offer at least the minimum wage.

Use the same resources to look for placements as you would to find an internship. Focus on smaller, independent companies in the local area, as these are more likely to offer short-term placements. Usually they will give you more of a free rein than you might get in a large, corporate company, and you will get an insight into how the company runs on all levels and throughout the different departments. Let the employer know what you are interested in before you start, and they should offer you some interesting jobs to work on.

VOLUNTEERING

There are plenty of ways you can volunteer your time, from nature conservation and caring for wildlife to teaching in schools or working in hospitals. There is also the option of volunteering in different parts of the world, although this is usually better done during a gap year. It is a great way to show you are a compassionate and hard-working person, and can help boost your CV with real working-life scenarios together with examples of when you used essential transferable skills.

Research companies first in order to make sure they have some sort of work experience programme, and then send a speculative email to them, stating why you want to volunteer, what your work experience is to date, and how you'd be an asset to the team. If the company is hot on their work experience scheme, they will probably have information on how you should apply on their website.

WORK SHADOWING

This is the perfect opportunity to see what a job entails before you set your heart and soul on making it your career. Shadowing only lasts one or two days, which should allow enough time to give you a flavour of the day-to-day duties required in that particular role. However, it does take up a lot of the employer's time and these opportunities are rarely advertised.

This means that you will have to send a speculative email in the first instance, or, if you have a connection with someone in the company, you could try contacting them first, as you are more likely to get a response. Unfortunately, it's likely that you won't hear back from a lot of corporate companies due to the sheer volume of similar emails they'll receive. You're likely to have a better chance contacting smaller independent businesses.

If you are successful, make sure you don't waste their time: prepare suitable questions in advance and try hard to make a good impression. If you liked what you saw during work shadowing, this could be an opportunity to see if they'd consider letting you do some work experience there.

BEHAVE DURING YOUR WORK EXPERIENCE PLACEMENT

Professional work experience can be daunting if you've never had a job before, or if your part-time role is one that doesn't require a huge amount of propriety. Here are some key ways to impress your employer:

TOP TIPS

- **Be enthusiastic and smile:** If you are bright and enthusiastic from the outset, this might encourage your manager to offer you more interesting jobs. It will also help them remember you – you never know when you might get a call about a vacancy that's just become available.

- **Ask questions:** If you don't understand something, then ask a colleague to help you. It might be that you don't understand a certain acronym (there are many specific to different industries), or a task you have been set. Instead of doing the wrong thing to begin with, and potentially putting yourself in a poor light, ask for clarification or for your colleague to explain a little more about the task they've given you.

- **Be bold (in a good way):** Sometimes it's worth organising a brief meeting with your manager (if they haven't already arranged this) on your first day at the company to give you a better idea of how it runs. If you want to see what it's like in several departments, a meeting is a good place to ask about this and give you a greater opportunity to learn about the industry. Making this sort of request will also show the manager that you have initiative.

- **Be true to yourself:** Work experience is the perfect way to find out if the company you are with is the sort of company you would like to work for in the future. Remember to check with yourself every so often to see if you are actually enjoying the work. Of course, all jobs have some dull tasks attached to them, and this will be even more evident during work experience, so weigh up a list of pros and cons in order to make your decision.

- **Know when to ask for more:** As mentioned above, you may have to perform some dull tasks during your work experience. However, if all you're doing is making tea and twiddling your thumbs, speak to your manager politely and ask if there is anything else they would like you to help with. If you don't feel you're making the most out of your time there, it's best to let them know as diplomatically as possible.

WRITE A CV

Your curriculum vitae (CV) should cover your education, work experience and skills over two pages of A4.

Start with your personal details, such as your name, address and contact details, and then write a short profile summary of yourself, for example:

I am a psychology graduate with experience in PR and marketing. As a natural communicator, I can interact with clients effectively and I can create and deliver campaigns that meet clients' business objectives. I am keen to develop my management and people skills.

When writing about your work experience you should put it in reverse chronological order, showing your most recent work positions first. This should be followed by your academic background and education achievements, then your skills and additional achievements, such as knowledge of a foreign language or ability to competently use relevant IT programmes. Finally, you can add your interests or hobbies, but only if there is enough space. Make sure you include as many relevant details as you can, including dates, so that the employer is as well-informed as possible.

Present details of your responsibilities and achievements in previous jobs in a concise and compelling way. If you are seeking a creative job, try to think about how you can present your CV to reflect your artistic personality. Where possible, show a connection between your interests and the nature of the job to demonstrate your fitness. For example, if you're applying for a job in fashion, reference your styling blog or portfolio.

Format your CV and use bulleted lists so that it's simple and easy to read, making sure you choose a professional-looking font.

Rather than writing just one CV, tailor the content to highlight your suitability for each job that you apply for.

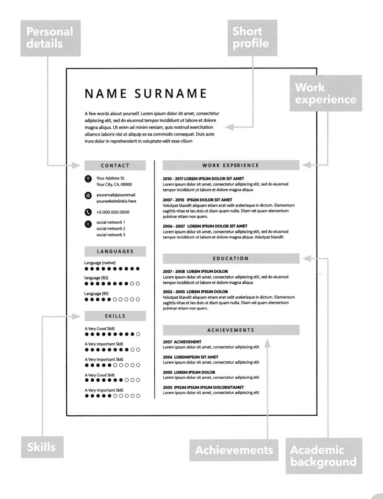

WRITE A COVERING LETTER

Although many jobs these days involve online applications, sending your CV and a covering letter to companies, either by email or by post, is still a common part of the application process.

For your covering letter, follow the rules for formal letter writing (search online for more information on this) and always quote the job reference in the header to clarify which job you are applying for. The letter needn't be long; in fact employers prefer letters that are clear and concise rather than long and rambling. Your covering letter needs to supplement your CV by focusing on why you want the job, as well as your suitability and enthusiasm for the role. Find a way to reference a positive fact about the company so it shows you're up-to-date about its values and goals.

If you're not confident about spelling or grammar, ask someone to proofread your letter before you send it off.

If you are submitting an unsolicited application – for example, if you want to see if they offer work experience – do your research on the company first. Ring up to find out who you should to write to and address them by name in your letter. If you don't, you risk the possibility your letter could go straight in the bin (or junk mail/trash).

INTERVIEW WELL

Whether you're doing your interview online or face-to-face, treat it seriously and, most importantly, do your research beforehand to demonstrate that you are really interested in the position and that you know what the company does. Practise delivering some answers before the interview, either with a friend or family member or alone to your bathroom mirror. Be clear on why you'd be an asset to the company and make your answers succinct.

If you are being interviewed online, choose a quiet room where there will be no interruptions. Set up your device so that you will have a plain background behind you, with nothing rude, lewd or 'immature' in shot. Position the camera so you can be seen from the waist up. Test all aspects of your tech before the interview. Make eye contact with the camera, sit up straight and don't talk too fast.

Dress in a style appropriate for the company or organisation you hope to join. If you're doing a face-to-face interview, arrive early and don't be spotted checking your phone while you're waiting to be called in. Ensure that it's switched off before you arrive.

Group interviews are often conducted to see how you might work with others as a team. Make sure you listen to what's going on and that you are seen to say something. Dilemmas may be posed to test how you might handle a client or customer query; your approach to resolving the issue might be more important than knowing the 'right' solution.

If you feel your nerves getting the better of you, take a deep breath and compose yourself. Although it may not seem like it, the people interviewing you are probably just as nervous as you are. You can always ask the interviewers to rephrase the question if you don't understand it, or if you want some time to think how to answer.

NEGOTIATE A PAY RISE

You don't have to be the modern-day Albert Einstein to be worth something to a company. As you spend longer working, you'll experience the other side of hiring and see just how tricky it is to find someone who works well and fits in with the company. So don't be afraid to negotiate.

However…

- **DON'T** negotiate at the interview as you haven't got the job yet and you don't want to come across as too arrogant.

- **DO** put your requests in context. Refer to the salary not reflecting the requirements of the role, for example.

- **DON'T** try to negotiate without having done your research. Simply saying, 'I want more money because I want more money' won't cut it.

- **DO** talk about precedent. Mention the average wage of people in your role in your area, if that would be helpful, or discuss the incentives that your current company offers, such as flexitime.

WRITE A PROFESSIONAL EMAIL

You may not be familiar with sending a ton of emails every day, but at most work places this will be required of you. Emails to colleagues and clients definitely aren't the same as a WhatsApp conversation with your friends, so to start you off on the right track, here are some essential dos and don'ts:

DO:

- Structure the message with an opening and closing greeting.

- Consider who the recipient is – if they are a client or someone external, make sure they will understand the terminology you are using, and that the tone of your email is more formal than if you were sending it to a co-worker.

- Follow up decisions that were made over the phone or face-to-face with an email summarising the key points discussed.

- Make the subject line concise and meaningful so that it is easily searchable should you or the recipient need to refer back to it.

- Check and correct spelling and grammar.

- If you need to set a deadline, make it stand out. Put it at the beginning of the email and format it in bold.

- Check you'd be happy for your manager to see an email before sending it.

DON'T:

- Write in capitals – IT LOOKS ANGRY!

- Copy irrelevant people into your emails – cc'ing too many people is confusing and could look like a digital ambush.

- Send an angry email. If you aren't happy with something, write the reply in a separate document (to avoid sending by accident!) to abate your frustration, but then save it and review it when you've calmed down.

- Get into a game of email ping-pong – if you can see this starting to happen, organise a meeting to discuss the matter instead.

- Email anything confidential or to pass on bad (or good) news.

- Open suspicious emails – delete them immediately.

FINAL WORD

You've come to the end of the book, and hopefully you've learned a thing or two. You might find it handy to keep this book out for the duration of your time at university, as it has information in it that you can refer to at different stages. There's no pressure to remember *all* this 'stuff that students should know' straight away - that's why this book has been written!

From celebrations and stress to studying and preparing for the future, you'll learn and grow so much from the experience university offers to you that, afterwards, you will feel 100 per cent ready to explore brand new opportunities and the big wide world.

Seize the day!

INDEX

A NEW BEGINNING:

Choose your accommodation 8

Get started 25

Know what to expect 19

Make friends 23

Make small talk 21

Make your accommodation
 a home 28

Master the terminology 29

Organise your admin 26

Pack 10

Reach out in a crisis 32

Remember names 22

Select gadgets 12

Stop feeling lonely 27

Tackle anxiety 31

Transport your belongings 18

KNUCKLING DOWN:

Avoid distractions
 during lectures 39

Conduct yourself
 during lectures 38

Handle other classes 42

Make the most of seminars,
 workshops and labs 43

Organise your handouts 45

Pack for lectures 37

Prepare for lectures 36

Prepare for the start of term 34

Process information 44

Take notes during lectures 40

Take the best notes 41

Understand your lectures 35

ACING YOUR EXAMS:

Cope when you're
 running out of time 57

Cope with exam anxiety 50

Cope with exam insomnia 51

Eat properly during
 exam time 53

Plan your revision 47

Revise 48

Start your exam 55

Stay calm before and
 during an exam 54

Stop feeling so sluggish 52

Take the next steps when
 you think you've failed
 your exam 58

Use your spare time 56

WRITING KNOCKOUT ESSAYS AND DISSERTATIONS:

Carry out independent research 63

Choose an essay topic 60

Compile a bibliography 67

Complete your essay 70

Finish your dissertation on time 72

Overcome writer's block 66

Pinpoint the relevant sections 62

Proofread your work 69

Read what you've written from an objective viewpoint 68

Start researching subjects 61

Start thinking about your dissertation 71

Structure essay 64

FOOD FOR THOUGHT:

Avoid cooking too much 78

Balance your diet 76

Batch cook 79

Drink (relatively) healthily 86

Put out kitchen fires 88

Store your food 74

Use leftovers 75

Wash up by hand 87

HEALTHY BODY, HEALTHY MIND:

Create a first-aid kit 99

Exercise at home 91

Exercise on a budget 90

Maintain your health 100

Perform basic first-aid 93

HOME, SWEET HOME:

Bleed a radiator 126

Change a fuse 119

Change a lightbulb 120

Choose your housemates 102

Clean a microwave 110

Clean a toilet 111

Clean an oven 109

Clean your kitchen 108

Create a fair cleaning rota 105

Do the laundry 116

Enjoy a no-drama houseshare 104

Fix a leaky pipe 127

Pack away bedsheets 114

Recycle 121

Remove stains from
  clothes/furniture   115
Select the best
  cleaning products   107
Unblock a drain   124

MONEY, MONEY, MONEY:

Budget   130
Cut back on spending   131
Earn money while
  studying   136
Find a cheap
  student house   129
Find a part-time job   135
Find cheap travel and
  accommodation when
  booking a holiday   137
Find discounts   132
Save money   133
Save money on toiletries   138

WORD HARD, PLAY HARDER:

Be safe on a night out   153
Cure a hangover   156
Get a date   165
Have a good
  fresher's week   140
Make the most of
  free time   164

Organise a first date   166
Pace yourself   150
Pick a fancy-dress outfit 142
Take a break from partying 162
Throw a house party   158
Tidy up after a party   161

GETTING A REAL JOB:

Behave during your work
  experience placement   176
Find work experience
  opportunities   173
Interview well   181
Negotiate a pay rise   182
Pick the right employability
  activities in your final year 172
Pick the right employability
  activities in your first year 170
Pick the right employability
  activities in your
  second year   171
Pursue your career path   169
Research your career
  options   168
Write a covering letter   180
Write a CV   178
Write a professional email 183

LIFE SKILLS

Julia Laflin

Paperback

ISBN: 978 1 78685 283 0

£9.99

COULD YOU MAKE A FIRE?
ARE YOU ABLE TO SEW ON A BUTTON?
DO YOU KNOW HOW TO NEGOTIATE A PAY RISE?

If the answer to any of the above is 'no', then don't worry – this book is here to give you a helping hand. Full of useful advice and practical skills that everyone should know, it will provide you with the essential knowledge you need to tackle life's everyday challenges. From the little things, like how to boil an egg or treat a blister, right up to the big things, like speaking in public, this handy guide will arm you with all the skills you need to navigate life in the real world like a pro.

IMAGE CREDITS

Have you enjoyed this book?
If so, why not write a review on
your favourite website?

If you're interested in finding out more
about our books, find us on Facebook at
Summersdale Publishers and follow
us on Twitter at **@Summersdale**.

Thanks very much for buying this
Summersdale book.

www.summersdale.com